T0267261

AROUND THE
OCEAN
IN
80
FISH

& OTHER SEA LIFE

For Claire, Dipali, Nancy and Nicole,
my dearest friends for the longest time.

LAURENCE KING

First published in Great Britain in 2023
by Laurence King an imprint of
The Orion Publishing Group Ltd,
Carmelite House,
50 Victoria Embankment,
London EC4Y 0DZ

An Hachette UK Company

10 9 8 7 6 5 4 3 2 1

Text © 2023 Helen Scales
Illustrations © 2022 Marcel George

A CIP catalogue record for this book is available from
the British Library.

Senior editor: Katherine Pitt
Design: Masumi Briozzo
Cover illustrations: Marcel George

ISBN: 978-1-39960-278-5

Origination by DL Imaging, UK
Printed in China by C&C Offset Printing Co. Ltd

www.laurenceking.com
www.orionbooks.co.uk

AROUND THE
OCEAN
IN
80
FISH

& OTHER SEA LIFE

Dr Helen Scales

Illustrated by Marcel George

Laurence King Publishing

Contents

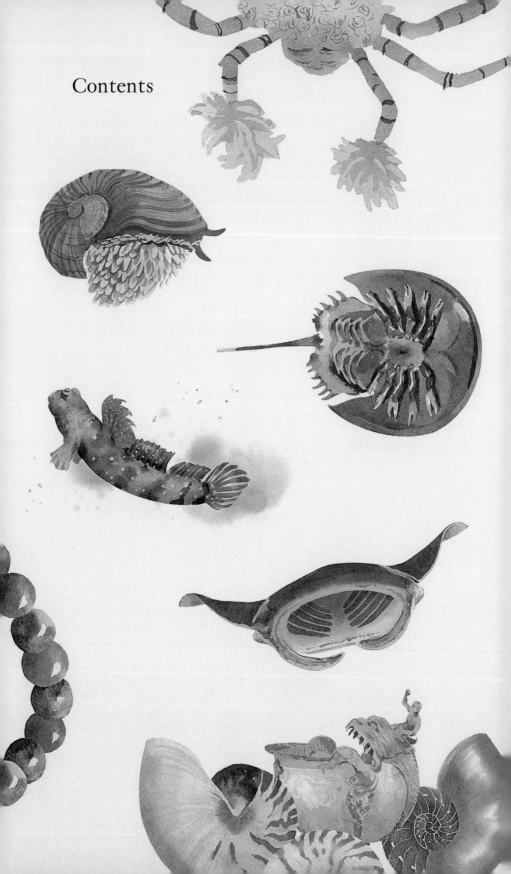

PACIFIC OCEAN

Introduction

This world that we call Earth is a water planet. Seven-tenths of the surface is covered in a vast, deep ocean. More than 90 per cent of the Earth's biosphere – the space where life dwells – is ocean. So, what better way to travel around the world than by following the animals that roam the coasts and open seas, into the greatest depths? That's more or less what I've been doing throughout my time as a marine biologist, a diver and an oceanographer in a quite literal sense: I write about the ocean (the word oceanography derives from ancient Greek words meaning ocean and writing). The very first time I jumped in with an air tank fixed to my back and saw a single, small, unassuming silvery fish right in front of me, my perspective on the world suddenly shifted. Since then, I've followed any fish I can find and a myriad of their aquatic companions, driven by an urge to know more about them, to find ways of protecting them from human-caused harm, and simply to watch them going about their liquid lives.

The ocean is full of wonders and surprises. All through this enormous, three-dimensional realm, organisms have taken on colours, shapes and behaviours that we just don't see here on land. The ocean has much to tell us about our biodiverse planet and how it thrives in many ways far beyond our own experiences as earth-walking, air-breathing mammals. There's a kaleidoscope of life waiting to be explored.

Selecting just 80 species for this aquatic tour of our planet was not an easy task. There are hundreds of thousands of known ocean-going animals to pick from, and many that I'm incredibly fond of. I could easily have filled the book just with species that scientists discovered in the ocean while I was writing it. Instead, I've done my best to curate a collection of animals that embody my ideas of what ocean life is really like. I want to show you the strange, hidden and beguiling things that go on beneath the waves, and occasionally above and beyond them, and even introduce some life forms that you might never have heard about. I also want to show you some of the more surprising aspects of well-known species, and to reflect on how scientists are constantly learning more about the living ocean's inner workings and how everything fits together.

All the animals in this book share a common habit of living in saltwater. Many of them we can legitimately call fish because they all belong to the same sprawling branches of the evolutionary tree; they have backbones and fins, most of them breathe water through gills and a lot of them have bodies covered in scales. They're joined by all sorts of animals that at one time or another people have called fish – a catch-all term for things that live in the sea, from whales and dolphins to jellyfish, starfish and cuttlefish.

I present them to you as occupants of a set of ocean basins: the Pacific, Indian and Atlantic Oceans, and the Mediterranean and polar seas. In reality, these are not separate spaces set apart by physical boundaries, but rather components of an interconnected global ocean that's mixed by restless currents and great underwater rivers. It takes a water molecule a thousand years on average to circumnavigate the entire globe. Many of the animals you're about to meet go on their own global journeys, migrating thousands of miles between breeding and feeding grounds, to find the resources and conditions they need to survive. To those I have allocated an ocean with which they are most strongly associated and in which they spend most time. Others stay put and can be seen only in particular places.

In this book, I've brought together animals that also reflect how human cultures have always been connected to ocean life in enduring and often unexpected ways. This is a part of our world that humans can still visit only briefly. Mostly, we stand at the edges of the sea and gaze over the waves, pondering and dreaming about what lies below. We catch glimpses of animals that live between the tides and others whose remains wash up on the drift line. Everything else lies hidden out of sight and out of mind, yet there are critical links between ocean life and our lives on land.

The ocean has fed people for millennia. Remains of 23,000-year-old fishhooks and piles of preserved fish bones dating back 42,000 years provide the oldest known evidence that humans were not only eating seafood easily gleaned along shorelines but also fishing far from shore, catching pelagic fish such as tuna. As well as extracting food, people have explored the ocean, discovered all manner of aquatic products and materials, and found for them great use and value. The seas have provided endless unique and strange substances, from shark fins and fake unicorn horns to silk woven from the golden threads of seashells and wave-worn lumps of sperm-whale poo.

Right now, people are increasingly looking to the ocean and ocean life for new ideas to solve human problems. Glowing jellyfish have revolutionized the way scientists study genes, cells, bodies and diseases. Deadly seashells produce a mind-numbing array of powerful chemicals that are tweaked and tamed to make new medicines. Engineers are seeking inspiration for the next generations of materials among animals that thrive in extreme conditions in the ocean's greatest depths.

As scientists find out ever more about the ocean and what lives there, it's also becoming increasingly clear that all life on Earth depends on a healthy ocean. The ocean provides countless critical but unseen services. Half the oxygen we breathe comes from plankton and algae in the surface seas that are fed by the deep ocean and nutrients sweeping up from below. The ocean plays a huge role in the global climate, soaking up vast quantities of heat and carbon and making the planet habitable. But all of that, and so much more in the ocean, is at risk.

There is a long history of people treating the ocean as if it were an infinite store cupboard. At the same time, the ocean is seen as a bottomless repository that will swallow all of humanity's unwanted waste. Now we know that neither is true. So many human impacts mingle in the ocean: industrial fishing, the flood of plastics and other persistent pollutants, habitats destroyed thoughtlessly or on purpose, and the problems of warming, rising, stormier seas.

The hopeful news is that gradually more people are shifting their mindset and realizing that the ocean is not too big to break. We must do whatever we can to make it as healthy, intact and diverse as possible, and we have better ideas than ever about how to do that. There is no single solution that will save the ocean, no silver bullet that will work everywhere. Ultimately, it will come down to people grasping the reality that the ocean is finite, precious and irreplaceable, and taking all sorts of action around the world. A crucial part of that is simply to know more, to be interested and to care more about ocean life, and that is how I hope this book will help.

Here is my selection of 80 fish and other marine animals, a gathering of envoys from the ocean that have their own stories to tell of life underwater and why the ocean matters. I hope you enjoy getting to know them.

Flapper Skate

Dipturus intermedius

In a Scottish aquarium in 2020, a flapper skate wriggled out of its egg case, unfurled its wings and began flapping around its tank. The pup was 27 centimetres (10½ in) long, showing why this species became critically endangered in the wild. From the moment they're born, flapper skates are big enough to be snagged easily by fishing nets and trawls.

This was the first of these giant, flattened relatives of sharks to be born in captivity. A pregnant flapper skate had been accidentally caught by fishermen and laid her egg on deck before they had a chance to let her go. The egg hatched 535 days later.

Flappers are the biggest skates in the Atlantic Ocean. Adults can spread their wings over 2 metres (6½ ft), which is approaching the size of a manta ray. They were formerly known as common skates, but that name was ditched when scientists identified two separate species: the flapper and blue skates. By then it was obvious that these skates were anything but common.

The only remaining stronghold for flapper skates is off the Shetland and Orkney islands, and the west coast of Scotland. In 2015 and 2021 two marine reserves were set up to protect areas that are important for the species. This includes a nursery site off the Isle of Skye, where divers found 100 flapper skate egg cases nestled among rocks and seaweed on the seabed.

People have known about Atlantic and North Sea skates for hundreds of years. In the sixteenth century there was a trade across Europe in 'Jenny Hanivers'. The name allegedly stems from the French *jeune fille d'Anvers*, 'young girl of Antwerp', suggesting that these creatures often came from the Belgian port. Sailors made these grotesque objects from dead skates and sold them as dragons, devils, mermaids or, rather unbelievably, angels. A skate's nostrils and mouth were fashioned into a Jenny Haniver's face, and a male skate's dangling, penis-like claspers became the legs.

These days, people are more likely to collect empty skate egg cases that have washed up on beaches. Egg case hunts have become an important way for citizen scientists to help track populations of flappers and other skates and egg-laying sharks.

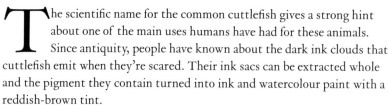

Common Cuttlefish

Sepia officinalis

The scientific name for the common cuttlefish gives a strong hint about one of the main uses humans have had for these animals. Since antiquity, people have known about the dark ink clouds that cuttlefish emit when they're scared. Their ink sacs can be extracted whole and the pigment they contain turned into ink and watercolour paint with a reddish-brown tint.

Cuttlefish ink had its heyday in the eighteenth and nineteenth centuries, when artists including J.M.W. Turner and Vincent van Gogh used sepia in their pen-and-wash drawings. It's possible to make ink not only from the sacs of recently killed cuttlefish but also from the preserved remains of their ancestors. In 1826 the British palaeontologist Mary Anning found a fossil belemnite, an extinct relative of cuttlefish, containing its original ink sac still filled with melanin-rich pigments. Her friend and fellow fossil collector Elizabeth Philpot mixed the fossilized pigment with water and used it to paint pictures of ichthyosaur fossils that were found in the same 200-million-year-old rocks as the ancient ink-bearing cephalopod.

Sepia photographs, on the other hand, have nothing to do with cuttlefish – except in their colour. The brown monotone photographs popular in Victorian times aren't faded black-and-white pictures, but were made by a chemical process in darkrooms that produced these sepia tones.

Cuttlefish use their ink for defence, squirting a dark cloud to startle an attacker. Other cephalopods make ink, including squid and octopuses. Sticky mucus mixed with the ink creates a blob in the water known as a pseudomorph, which may act as a decoy while the real cuttlefish gets away. Spotty bobtail squid make strands of ink 'rope' five times the length of their body (only around 1 cm), which they hold on to and hide among, perhaps masquerading as a clump of drifting seagrass leaves.

There are more than 100 cuttlefish species, including Australian giant cuttlefish (*Sepia apama*), which grow to more than 1 metre (3 ft) long and weigh 10 kilograms (22 lb); striped pyjama squid (*Sepioloidea lineolata*), actually a cuttlefish; and flamboyant cuttlefish (*Metasepia pfefferi*) – flamboyant being both their official name and an accurate description of their stunning appearance and flickering colours.

The white, oval cuttlebones that wash up on beaches are the cuttlefishes' spongy internal shells, which serve a similar purpose to the chambered nautilus shell, boosting their buoyancy. When cuttlefish die, their 'bones' float to the surface and often get swept on to shore. Historically, people have collected them and ground them down to use as polishing powders and as an additive for toothpaste. Being made of calcium carbonate, cuttlebones have even been used as an antacid. A traditional metal casting technique uses cuttlebones as moulds. A ring pressed between two pieces of cuttlefish bone will leave an impression that can be filled with molten metal to make a replica. Nowadays, people who keep birds and chinchillas, and even hermit crabs and snails, give their pets cuttlebones to gnaw on and supplement the calcium in their diet.

Like various of their cephalopod relatives, cuttlefish are showing themselves to be impressively smart. In a recent study carried out at Cambridge University, common cuttlefish demonstrated that they can exert remarkable self-control. They passed a version of the marshmallow test, in which human children are offered either one marshmallow now or two if they're prepared to wait a while. Instead of marshmallows, cuttlefish were offered pieces of prawn, which they could eat right away if they wanted, or they could opt for the more delicious live shrimp. But they could have the shrimp only if they waited and didn't eat the prawn. In the tests, cuttlefish did indeed wait for the tastier snack, for more than two minutes. The cuttlefish even turned their back on the prawns, deliberately resisting temptation while waiting for the tastier snacks to come along. This ability to delay gratification is a sign that cuttlefish are good at decision-making and planning for the future.

ATLANTIC

Sturgeon

Acipenseridae

Most people have never seen a fully grown sturgeon – with rows of bony plates called scutes instead of scales, and dangling moustaches called barbels – but many are familiar with these fish at a much earlier stage in life. Sturgeon eggs have long been an epicurean delight. The ancient Greek philosopher Aristotle spoke highly of caviar. The delicacy gained popularity in the nineteenth century, when the French started importing it from Russia, and in the early twentieth century American caviar flooded the global market. It was so cheap that it was given away as a salty bar snack, like peanuts, to encourage patrons to drink more.

Still today, hundreds of tonnes of caviar are produced and eaten each year, largely from farmed rather than wild sturgeon. Most highly prized is caviar from beluga sturgeon (*Huso huso*), a giant species from the Caspian and Black seas. At up to 8 metres (26 ft) long, they can outsize their mammalian namesake, beluga whales. In 1924 a female beluga sturgeon caught in Russia weighed 1.2 tonnes, including almost a quarter tonne of eggs. The species is now critically endangered owing to over-fishing and poaching. The same goes for the starry and diamond sturgeons (*Acipenser stellatus* and *A. gueldenstaedtii*), two species that have become a vanishingly rare sight across their former ranges in the Black, Azov and Caspian seas. Their eggs are prized, respectively, as sevruga and ossetra caviar. The sturgeon family as a whole is not doing well, with 23 out of 27 species at risk of extinction. Dams blocking migration paths to the sturgeons' spawning grounds are also taking their toll on populations.

As well as their eggs, there's another, somewhat lesser-known body part of sturgeons that people have been extracting and using for centuries. Like many fish, sturgeons have a gas-filled swim bladder that helps them control their buoyancy. A sturgeon's thin-skinned bladder is more or less the right shape and size to be made into condoms, which were tied in place with ribbons. Fish condoms were used in Europe in the seventeenth century and handed out to soldiers in the English Civil War to reduce the spread of syphilis. A more enduring and widespread use of sturgeon swim bladders is to make a transparent substance called isinglass. Isinglass was used as glue in ancient Egypt, and the Romans used it to seal wounds and mend broken bones. There are reports of Roman entertainers smearing it on their feet to stop themselves from getting burned when they walked over hot coals.

Centuries later, British brewers began using isinglass. The high collagen content causes yeast in beer to clump together and sink out of suspension, resulting in a clear, sparkling pint. This became especially important when ceramic and metal beer tankards were replaced by glass. Originally, Russian sturgeon isinglass was used. It came as a by-product of the caviar trade. Then, in the mid-eighteenth century, cheaper swim bladders from cod were found to work just as well. Some brewers still use isinglass today. As recently as 2017, trace amounts were still found in every pint of Guinness.

Western Europe has its own species of sturgeon, one that – like its easterly cousins – is critically endangered. European sturgeon have been hunted for centuries, mainly for their meat. In a similar way to salmon, they spend most of their lives at sea before migrating up rivers to spawn inland. In times gone by they spawned in huge aggregations. This spectacle was last seen in France's Gironde estuary in 1994. Over the past few decades, efforts have been made to boost populations. Approximately 1.6 million sturgeon fry were reared in captivity and released into the wild between 2007 and 2015. It takes males 12 years to reach maturity, and females 20 years, so those that have survived should soon be ready to mate. Fisheries scientists are keeping a close eye out because any day now the captive-bred sturgeon could start reappearing in spawning grounds across Europe.

Limpet

Patellidae

L impets are unassuming sea snails. Some might call them boring, but
it really depends on when you encounter them. Limpets have learned
to survive in an ever-changing world. Over the course of a day, as the
tide rises and falls, they cope with cold water and crashing waves, followed
by exposure to dry air and the possibility of being boiled by the sun.

Limpets are easiest to see when the tide is out, but that's also when
they're at their most private and hidden. They look like small, inert
volcanoes. A limpet clamps its shell tightly to a rock, using a combination
of its muscly foot acting as a suction cup and a sticky goo to glue itself
temporarily in place. This stops the snail from drying out and makes it
difficult for a hungry seabird to peck it off. To dislodge a limpet from a rock
can take a force of 100 kilograms (220 lb).

As the tide comes in, limpets wake up and search for food. They scrape
at young seaweed sporelings with their sandpapery tongue, like a cat licking
a bowl of frozen milk. If you're prepared to get wet feet and explore a rocky
shore carefully as the tide comes in, sneak up and lower your ear to a limpet-
strewn rock. You might hear them chewing.

Look out too for the geometric artworks limpets draw across rocks.
The zigzag trails are testament to the extraordinarily tough teeth that
cover their tongues. A team of materials scientists discovered that the
secret to their super strength lies in masses of tiny tubes made of an
iron-rich mineral called goethite. Limpet teeth are the toughest known
biological material. Should it want to, a limpet could chew its way through
a bulletproof vest.

Scientists have also investigated the gleaming stripes on blue rayed
limpets – the most dazzling limpet species. Their shells contain thin layers
with a disorderly structure that reflects blue light in ways that could inspire
uses in the human world, such as transparent optical displays projected on
to car windscreens.

Another limpet mystery remains unsolved. When the tide drops, they
head straight back to the spot they call home. For now, nobody quite knows
how a limpet never gets lost.

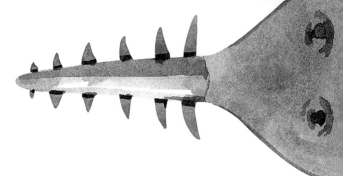

Sawfish

Pristis spp.

I t's a rare event, these days, to glimpse the toothed snout of a wild sawfish. They used to roam coastlines across the world in more than 90 countries, where they inspired all sorts of beliefs. But it was the very body part that spawned these myths and legends that also led to the sawfishes' downfall. Their impressive spiky snouts, officially called rostrums, serve a dual purpose as a probe, sensing minute electromagnetic signals from prey, and as a weapon to slash and kill. The rostrum can make up as much as a quarter of a sawfish's body length and all too easily gets snagged in fishing nets.

A tour of world art, folk stories and artefacts shows how for millennia people have embraced sawfish as supernatural powers, warriors, protectors and bringers of good fortune. In ancient ruins of the Aztec empire, tombs have been found with offerings of sawfish rostrums. These ritual objects were perhaps used in human sacrifice, or as offerings to the gods. Ancient pottery of the Coclé people of Panama, from 1,400 years ago, features stylized sawfish, and these creatures are still significant for indigenous people in Panama today. The Kuna, who live in the San Blas archipelago off the Panama coast, believe that sawfish protect them against dangerous sea creatures and save people from drowning, and shamans summon the help of golden sawfish spirits.

According to the Anindilyakwa people of the Northern Territory of Australia, ancestral sawfish carved out rivers with their toothy saws. In the Sepik River in Papua New Guinea, native people believe sawfish spirits will punish those who break fishing taboos, by unleashing terrible rainstorms. In Borneo, the scholar who brought Islam to the island is known as Tuan Tunggang Parangan, 'Mr Sawfish Rider', because it's said he arrived on the back of a huge sawfish.

Seen as 'sharks with swords', sawfish have commonly been linked with warfare. Their rostrums were used as traditional weapons in the Philippines, Papua New Guinea, Senegal and even New Zealand, where the species never naturally occurred. In Iran, sawfish have been found in ruins dating back 6,000 years, and they were depicted as an animal swordsman, a symbol of warriors. Much more recently, during World War II, Nazi U-boats and an American submarine were adorned with sawfish insignia.

In the Bijagos archipelago in Guinea-Bissau, West Africa, young men perform dances wearing triangular wooden masks that were once topped with the rostrum of a young sawfish; as sawfish disappeared from the wild, wooden models began to be used instead. Dancers in Nigeria wear life-size sawfish masks, mimicking the benevolent water spirits they believe bestow wealth and good fish catches. In Gambia, sawfish rostrums are hung up to protect houses from catastrophe and fires, and in cattle pens to protect livestock.

Today, the most common depictions of sawfish are on the coins and notes of the West African CFA franc, used in eight mostly coastal countries between Senegal and Benin. The design depicts one of the ancient bronze weights used centuries ago in Ghana to measure out the traditional currency of gold dust.

They may look like sharks with an additional, ferocious nosepiece, but sawfish are in fact rays, shark cousins within the elasmobranchs; you can tell because their gills are on the flattened underside of their bodies. They're sometimes mistaken for sawsharks, which have a similar toothed rostrum, but also a pair of barbels dangling down like a snooty moustache and gills on the side of their body, which show that they are, in fact, sharks. The fact that sawfish are not sharks doesn't stop them from being targeted for their fins to make into sharks'-fin soup. Populations of the five known species of sawfish have crashed in recent decades, mostly through overfishing. The only places where you have a shot at seeing one are Florida and northern Australia, where they're strictly protected.

European Eel

Anguilla anguilla

Eels are eternally mysterious fish. For thousands of years they've been surrounded by big questions, the most curious being *Where do eels come from?* Through the ages, people have put forward all sorts of ideas. In ancient Egypt, eels were said to be made by the sun warming the Nile. The ancient Greek philosopher Aristotle proposed that eels sprang spontaneously out of mud. Pliny the Elder suggested that they rubbed themselves on rocks, shedding bits of skin, which came to life as young eels.

That the origin of eels has been enigmatic for so long is perhaps surprising given how many of them people have eaten. These are European eels, one of 18 species in the genus *Anguilla*. In medieval England, eels were an important part of the economy. They were cheap food for the masses, caught with willow traps in rivers and lakes up and down the country. As well as tucking into eel pies and slurping eel broth, people often used eels to pay their rent. By the end of the eleventh century, more than half a million of these creatures were used as currency each year. Landlords who became known for taking eels as payment included the slippery animals on their family crests.

Eels continued to be popular food in England in the eighteenth and nineteenth centuries, including jellied eels, a dish that originated in London's East End and for a time was made from eels caught in the River Thames. Eels are naturally rich in gelatine, which is released when they're boiled in stock and then sets into solid jelly. The English aren't the only keen eaters of eels. European eels have been smoked in Germany, Poland and Denmark, braised in beer in Sweden, and cooked in tomato sauce in Italy and in a green herby sauce in Belgium.

But the mystery of eels continued. As recently as the mid-nineteenth century, old ideas were still circulating that eels began their lives as beetles. As ridiculous as this may sound, eels are amazing shapeshifters and alter their appearance radically throughout their lives. People eventually worked out that what were assumed to be several different animals are in fact all eels, of different ages and life stages.

There are transparent wrigglers, like glassy bootlaces, known as elvers or glass eels. Much bigger are the yellow eels that are found inland, often in ponds and lakes. Silver eels are the ones people saw swimming along rivers towards the sea. Those are three key stages in the life cycle of eels, but still puzzles remain.

Sigmund Freud, the founder of psychoanalysis, worked earlier in his scientific career on a rather different animal from humans. In the 1870s he spent long hours at his dissecting table hoping to become the first person to see an eel's testicles. He couldn't find any, and thanks to the later work of a Danish scientist we now know why.

Johannes Schmidt, like many before him, became captivated by the question of where eels come from. For 20 years he scoured the Atlantic for eel larvae, and in 1923 he published a paper pinpointing their source to the Sargasso Sea, a huge region near Bermuda. His theory is that eels migrate there to spawn. Their larvae, which look like tiny leaves with tiny heads, have been found drifting from the Sargasso Sea to Europe (American eels, *A. rostrata*, spawn in the same area and drift west as larvae). On reaching the coast of Europe, the larvae transform into glass eels. Older, yellow eels migrate inland along rivers, where they stay for decades before transforming one last time into silver eels and swimming thousands of miles back to their birthplace, maturing on the way. Finally, in 2022, British scientists tracked mature female silver eels with satellite tags swimming all the way to the Sargasso Sea, just as Schmidt had predicted.

Today, the big question is what the future holds for eels. In recent decades the number of glass eels along European coasts has plummeted by more than 95 per cent. European eels are now critically endangered. The decline is linked to dams blocking their migration paths along rivers, and to a billion-dollar illegal eel trade. Demand for eels in Asian cuisine is not met by the local species, Japanese eels (*A. japonica*), and eels don't breed in captivity. Eel-smuggling gangs make huge profits trafficking wild-caught European glass eels to be reared in fish farms in Asia. Conservationists have called it the world's greatest wildlife crime.

Basking Shark

Cetorhinus maximus

N ever underestimate the abilities of basking sharks. Best known
as serene plankton suckers, they cruise around with their huge
mouths open, filtering tiny prey from the sea with seemingly
no need for great speed. And yet, if you follow one for long enough there's
a good chance it will suddenly launch its entire body out of the water.
Basking sharks can clear 1 metre (3 ft) or more of air above the waves, an
impressive feat for animals that can be more than 10 metres (33 ft) long and
weigh 3 or 4 tonnes. Being the world's second-largest fish they do, of course,
land with a considerable splash.

Analysing video of these aerial acrobatics, scientists have calculated
that leaping basking sharks swim at 18 kilometres an hour (11 mph) as they
shoot towards the surface. That's the same speed as great white sharks reach
when they perform similar stunts. It makes sense that great whites are able
to put on such a turn of speed, being active apex predators and chasing
fast-swimming prey, such as seals. In the case of basking sharks, it shows
that most of the time they choose to bask, but they can pick up the pace
considerably if they want to.

Why exactly basking sharks – and, for that matter, great whites –
expend so much energy leaping from the sea is another of the ocean's great
unsolved mysteries. Scientists have plenty of ideas about it. The sharks
could be sending messages to each other, showing off to mates, asserting
their dominance or perhaps dislodging itchy parasites from their skin.
Basking sharks also go on long journeys. One female was tagged with
a satellite tracker off the Isle of Man, then set off across the Atlantic,
swimming nearly 10,000 kilometres (6,215 miles) in less than three
months, ending up in Newfoundland, Canada. Sharks from Cape Cod
have swum to the mouth of the Amazon River, perhaps to reach mating and
pupping grounds.

Basking sharks used to be hunted for their huge, oily livers, which
are rich in vitamin A and squalene, a substance used to make industrial
lubricants and cosmetics. There have been fisheries in Norway, Scotland
and Ireland since the eighteenth century. In the 1940s, before writing
his bestselling book about otters, *Ring of Bright Water* (1960), the British
naturalist Gavin Maxwell attempted to set up a basking-shark fishery on
the Scottish isle of Soay. He wrote about his experiments in killing the

animals with machine guns, shotguns and harpoons, and described the gory challenge of extracting their livers from deep inside their bodies. At that time in Scotland, small bounties were paid to fishermen who killed basking sharks because these fish were considered pests. They damaged fishing nets by getting tangled in them, and back then people also thought basking sharks – with those enormous jaws – were scoffing all the valuable fish stocks. Similarly, the population of basking sharks off British Columbia in Canada was persecuted. Between 1955 and 1964 there was a federal eradication programme and a patrol vessel with a blade mounted on its bow, designed to slice basking sharks in half.

In most places, basking-shark fisheries collapsed when the populations were depleted and they were no longer easy to catch. It's thought that 100,000 were caught in the North Atlantic, even as late as the 1990s in the United Kingdom. The species is now largely protected from fishing, and numbers in the wild seem relatively stable. Some are still caught incidentally and their huge fins are highly valuable, not so much to make soup but to hang up as trophies.

Basking sharks probably explain many historical sea-monster fables. When their carcasses wash up naturally on beaches they can be in such a state of decomposition and disarticulation that people who find them quickly begin to conjure terrible beasts in their minds.

Atlantic Bluefin Tuna

Thunnus thynnus

Bluefin tuna are big, fast fish. They can grow to the size of small cars and swim at similar speeds, propelled by their sickle-shaped tail slicing through the water and powerful, red muscles heated by warm blood flowing around their bodies. The bluefin's formidable character is quite by chance what led to their fame today, as a symbol of swift ecological demise and also as a gourmet food. At the ceremonial fish auctions in Tokyo each January, individual bluefin tuna sell for extortionate prices. In 2019 the self-styled 'Tuna King', sushi restaurant owner Kiyoshi Kimura, paid 333.6 million yen (around $3 million) for just one fish. The new year auctions are a marketing stunt – prices throughout the rest of the year are never as high – yet this is a sign of the feverish popularity of bluefin tuna. But it hasn't always been that way.

Traditionally, Japanese people preferred milder, more subtle fish for their sushi, including white fish and shellfish, to the meaty taste of bluefin tuna. In the 1840s tuna was nicknamed *neko-matagi*, meaning 'even a cat would step over it'. A shift in attitudes to tuna originated in the 1950s a long way from Japan. In the United States and Canada, sport fishermen began to do battle with the mighty bluefin tuna that migrated seasonally along the Atlantic coast. These giant beasts were a favourite target for fishers to wrestle with on their enormous rods and reels. To win tournaments and show off prize catches, animals were brought ashore to be weighed and photographed, then the carcasses were usually thrown away. Tuna were tossed into landfill, thrown back into the sea and sometimes even sold to pet-food factories, but nobody in North America thought of eating them. The bloody meat was not to people's tastes.

This was around the time when Japanese electronics became hugely popular in the United States and were flown over the Pacific by the planeload. The downside was that those aeroplanes were flying home empty. Japanese Airlines hired a team to find a commodity in North America to fill the holds of their planes, and that is where the bluefins came in. One executive suggested they load up with the cheap frozen carcasses of bluefin tuna that sports fishers were throwing away, and try promoting them to sushi chefs. The initiative happened to coincide with a shift in Japanese palates, following World War II, when more people had started eating beef. The nation was primed for the meatier taste of bluefin tuna, and it took off. It wasn't long before the taste for bluefin tuna was exported from Japan back to the United States, and demand for the species went global. Within a few years bluefin had gone from junk fish to delicacy, all thanks to a clever marketing scheme.

There are three species of bluefin tuna. The Atlantic species is the biggest, then come the Pacific bluefins (*Thunnus orientalis*) and the southern bluefins (*T. maccoyii*), that live respectively in the North and South Pacific. All were targeted for the sushi trade, and all declined substantially as a result. For every 50 Atlantic bluefin tuna that were alive in 1940, only one was alive in 2010. Around that time, things got so bad for the wild bluefins that measures were brought in based on scientific advice to reduce the quotas that are allowed to be caught. The good news is that this seems to be working, and bluefin tuna are on a tentative road to recovery. Their numbers are still far lower than they were before commercial fishing began, but populations are slowly growing and Atlantic bluefin tuna is no longer considered endangered. On the global list of endangered species, the southern bluefin has been moved from the 'Critically Endangered' category to the less urgent 'Endangered', reflecting the increase in their numbers.

John Dory

Zeus faber

The John Dory is a curious-looking fish, with its crown of spines, its mottled bronze skin and a dark spot on either side of its flattened, upright body. Not a great deal is known about this species, which lives in warm seas worldwide and prowls around as a solitary, ambush hunter. Even more mysterious are the origins of both its common and scientific names. The eighteenth-century Swedish naturalist Carolus Linnaeus, the 'father of taxonomy', named the species in his vast book of life, *Systema naturae*. The genus, *Zeus*, is named after the ancient Greek god of the sky; *faber* means blacksmith and perhaps signifies the fish's black thumbprint.

Various stories tell of how the fish came to be known as John Dory, although none is altogether convincing. Some say it stems from the French words *jaune* and *dorée*, meaning yellow and golden, which makes some sense given the fish's gilded appearance, but why label it with a double name? The species also goes by the name of St Peter's fish in English, also *pesce San Pietro* in Italian, *pez San Pedro* in Spanish and *Petersfisch* in German. The black spot is allegedly where St Peter, the patron saint of fishermen, picked up the fish. A similar story is told of the dark smudge on the side of a haddock, although in some versions it's the devil who left his mark.

Wherever the name came from, John Dories are set to become a more common sight as the seas continue to warm. Fisheries scientists predict that cool-water species, such as cod, will increasingly move out of the North Sea and fish from warmer waters will take their place. In Britain, the nation's favourite dish could become John Dory and chips.

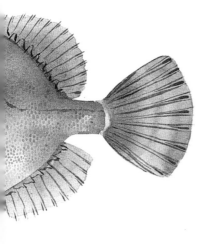

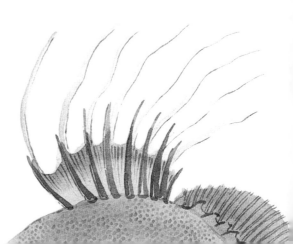

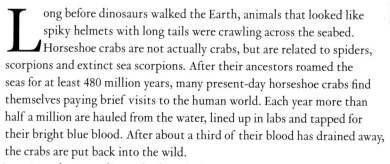

Atlantic Horseshoe Crab

Limulus polyphemus

L ong before dinosaurs walked the Earth, animals that looked like
spiky helmets with long tails were crawling across the seabed.
Horseshoe crabs are not actually crabs, but are related to spiders,
scorpions and extinct sea scorpions. After their ancestors roamed the
seas for at least 480 million years, many present-day horseshoe crabs find
themselves paying brief visits to the human world. Each year more than
half a million are hauled from the water, lined up in labs and tapped for
their bright blue blood. After about a third of their blood has drained away,
the crabs are put back into the wild.

Most humans alive today have had a potentially life-saving encounter
with the blood of a horseshoe crab. The blue comes from haemocyanin,
the equivalent of red haemoglobin in human blood. More importantly,
the blood of the horseshoe crab contains powerful immune cells, called
amoebocytes, which are highly sensitive to toxins made by bacteria.
Extracts of horseshoe crab blood are used to test the safety of new
medicines, surgical equipment and medical implants. Demand for
these tests for bacterial toxins has recently soared from developers
of coronavirus vaccines.

In the past, scientists assumed that most horseshoe crabs survived
their ordeal in the bleeding labs, but in fact studies have shown that as
many as one in three dies after release. Females often stop spawning. A
synthetic alternative to their blood has been available since around 2010,
but regulators are dragging their feet and uptake by pharmaceutical
companies is slow.

Horseshoe crabs face other threats, too. Asian tri-spine horseshoe
crabs, one of the four living species, are losing their spawning grounds
owing to coastal developments, pollution and rising sea levels. The
American species is heavily fished to make into bait for eel and whelk
fisheries. Their loss is bad news for other animals. In early summer,
thousands of horseshoe crabs crawl up the shore at Delaware Bay on the
east coast of the United States. Males cling to females as they lay eggs
in the sand. The eggs are critical food for migrating birds, including red
knot, which stop off on their journey from the tip of South America to the
Canadian Arctic. Without the horseshoe crab caviar to fuel them, the birds
wouldn't make it.

Pilot Whale

Globicephala spp.

More people get to see large numbers of pilot whales, both the long- and short-finned species, than any other species of cetacean. Sadly, that's because these marine mammals are notorious for stranding on coastlines, whole pods at a time. It's not uncommon to see pictures in the news of their slick black bodies lined up on the sand, usually with teams of rescuers working hard to save them and get them safely back out to sea. Their efforts don't always work. In 2020 close to 400 long-finned pilot whales died after beaching in Tasmania in one of Australia's worst strandings on record.

It continues to be a mystery why these agile, expert swimmers and underwater navigators so commonly get stuck in the shallows. Their strong social bonds are thought to be at least partly to blame. Pilot whales live in close-knit matriarchal pods, usually of between 10 and 30 animals, led by an older female. And if one member of the pod gets into trouble, the others will follow. In 2015, off the Isle of Skye in Scotland, a female pilot whale was having trouble giving birth and came towards the shore in great distress. The rest of her pod followed her onto the beach.

There are also well-known whale-stranding black spots, such as Farewell Spit in Golden Bay, New Zealand. Something about the geography and hydrology forms a whale trap, possibly as the tide races out leaving wide areas of shallow sea with a sloping sandy seabed that confuses the whales' echolocation system.

For centuries, people have known of the pilot whales' natural stranding behaviour and used it to their advantage during whale hunts. In the time of the Vikings, people hunted pilot whales in the Faroe Islands, and they still do today. When a pod of pilot whales is seen near shore, a flotilla of boats goes out and herds them in towards the beach. The whales are then slaughtered by hand in the shallows, turning the sea red. The hunters maintain that this is a tradition that provides important, sustainable food for people on an island that has very little land suitable for growing crops or rearing livestock, but animal-welfare groups label the hunt as cruel and unnecessary. There's similar condemnation of pilot-whale hunts in Japan.

Stranded and slaughtered pilot whales are revealing an unsettling truth about the health of the ocean. Pilot whales can live up to 60 years and accumulate toxins from their diet, including mercury, cadmium and other ocean-borne pollutants. Scientists have found that levels of toxins in the brains of stranded pilot whales increases with their age. Accordingly, in 2008 the chief medical officers in the Faroe Islands decided that pilot-whale meat was no longer fit for human consumption.

Cone Snail

Conidae

L ook, but don't touch. So the saying goes when exploring the sea, and for plenty of good reasons, including the beautiful but occasionally deadly cone snails. Some 700 species live in shallow tropical seas. They range from fingernail-sized miniatures to ones that would make a satisfying ice-cream cone, but not for licking, since each species makes a signature cocktail of toxins, known as conotoxins, which they load into their hollow teeth and spit out. Not many cone snails will do you much harm, but a few species are deadly to humans. The geography cone (*Conus geographus*) delivers a numbing tickle followed by swift paralysis of the diaphragm and eventually suffocation. And there's no anti-venom; conotoxins are far too complex for that. Between them, cone snails make an armoury of tens of thousands of unique chemicals.

Long before people uncovered the snails' chemical diversity, they were charmed by the ornate patterns of their shells. The remains of prehistoric artefacts indicate that people have collected and worn cone-snail shells for millennia. In more recent times, puka shell necklaces originally made in Hawaii from strings of sea-worn cone-shell fragments became a symbol of 1960s surfing counterculture that soon went mainstream.

Cone snails are a favourite of shell collectors because of these intricate patterns, which include dots, spots, stripes, triangles and zigzags. Behind all these patterns lies an unanswered mystery. Why do these snails have such decorative shells when they live hidden in sand, emerging only to hunt under cover of darkness? For now, nobody really knows. One possibility is that the patterns are markers that help the snails to make their shells. Snails expand their shells continuously as they grow, adding more shell material (calcium carbonate) to the open end. The patterns could help them align correctly and avoid growing a wonky shell.

We do know why and how these snails are so very dangerous. Most cone snails are vermivorous, which is to say they eat worms. The more dangerous species, remarkably, hunt fish. Their sophisticated chemical weaponry allows these slow crawlers to catch prey that would otherwise quickly wriggle or swim away. Recent studies have revealed that some conotoxins mimic the hormone insulin, causing fish to pass out from a sudden drop in blood sugar. Others mimic pheromones, hoodwinking the worms into a frenzied mass orgy, distracting them with the promise of sex and making them much easier to catch.

Just as cone snails copy their prey's natural molecules, so humans are copying conotoxins. A painkiller based on a conotoxin from the magical cone (*Conus magus*) blocks chronic pain signals to the brain. New conotoxin-inspired drugs in the pipeline include treatments for AIDS, COVID-19 and malaria, so it's likely that rather than killing, cone snails will soon be saving lives.

Hagfish

Myxini

If you've ever heard of hagfish, chances are you know about their party trick. Put one of these eel-like fish in a bucket, give it a quick stir and soon you will have a bucket full of slime. And not just any slime, but a remarkable material that's keeping scientists fascinated as they figure out how the hagfish do it.

For one thing, the hagfish can fill a bucket within a split second of releasing just a teaspoon of material through the hundred slime glands dotted along its body. They make a mixture of mucus and protein threads a hundred times thinner than human hair. Inside specialized cells, the threads coil into neat structures that look like pine cones. When released, these coils unspool rapidly and expand to 10,000 times their volume. The stretchy fibres are ten times stronger than nylon. Materials scientists are looking to hagfish slime to engineer bungee cords and protective fabrics, and the US Navy is interested in making artificial hagfish goo to bring enemy ships to a halt by surrounding them in a temporary, impenetrable sea of slime.

Hagfish evolved their exceptional slime as a means of defence. Film footage shot in the deep sea shows a shark attacking a hagfish, then quickly spitting it out as soon as it gets slimed. The goo clogs the gills of predators. Hagfish avoid choking themselves in their own slime with another clever trick: they tie their bodies in knots. Lacking a spine, they are very bendy and can loop themselves into an overhand knot, then slide it along their body, thus ridding themselves of the slime. They also do this when they're feeding, to help give them purchase against a carcass. Hagfish are scavengers. They clean up animal bodies – anything from fish to giant whales – that drop to the seabed. Lacking jaws, they can't take a bite, but they rasp at skin with rough plates on either side of their mouth. Hagfish will get inside a carcass through any hole they can, then they simply lie inside absorbing nutrients through their skin.

Around the world, hagfish are caught and shipped to Korea, where there's demand for leather made from their grey-pink, scaleless skin. People also eat them and have at times used the slime as a cooking ingredient, as an alternative to egg white. Hagfish have been fished out in the seas around Korea, so now they're imported from more distant waters. Off Australia, Brazil and Japan hagfish are at risk of becoming extinct. They may have

unappealing habits, but they play an important role in the oceans, clearing up carrion and helping to maintain rich seabed environments where other fish thrive.

Another group of jawless fish is the lampreys (Petromyzontiformes), some 38 parasitic species that suck the blood of other fish. Lampreys have a long history of people eating them. It's not clear whether King Henry I really did die from scoffing a 'surfeit of lampreys', as legend has it, but these fish have appeared for centuries in the cuisines of many countries, especially Europe. Since the Middle Ages, it's been a tradition for chefs in the English city of Gloucester to send a lamprey pie to the reigning monarch every year.

Hagfishes and lampreys can trace their ancestors directly back further than any other living fish, although which of them evolved first is a matter of debate. Despite their primeval beginnings, lampreys have a lot to teach scientists today. For one thing, if a lamprey's spinal cord is completely severed, the fish undergoes a spontaneous recovery and three months later is swimming around as if nothing happened. Lampreys can even recover if their spinal cord is cut in the same place a second time. Studies of the way lampreys regenerate their broken nerves are paving the way towards treatment for people with spinal-cord injuries.

Sperm Whale

Physeter macrocephalus

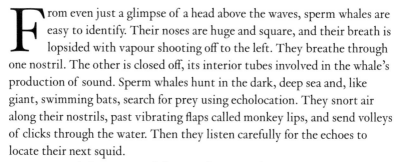

From even just a glimpse of a head above the waves, sperm whales are easy to identify. Their noses are huge and square, and their breath is lopsided with vapour shooting off to the left. They breathe through one nostril. The other is closed off, its interior tubes involved in the whale's production of sound. Sperm whales hunt in the dark, deep sea and, like giant, swimming bats, search for prey using echolocation. They snort air along their nostrils, past vibrating flaps called monkey lips, and send volleys of clicks through the water. Then they listen carefully for the echoes to locate their next squid.

Sperm whales are one of the ocean's species that people got to know well by hunting, butchering and processing millions of them. For centuries European and American whalers chased sperm whales in order to harvest various valuable body parts. The most important commodity was the golden liquid encased in their noses. It was named spermaceti because people wrongly thought it was sperm (now, it's thought spermaceti focuses the whales' beams of sound as they hunt). Whalers scooped hundreds of gallons of spermaceti from each sperm whale's enormous nose. It was valued highly as a fine oil that burns clear and bright. Spermaceti lit the streets of nineteenth-century Europe and America, and it was burned in the powerful lamps of lighthouses.

Whalers also searched inside sperm whales for another valuable product. Ambergris is the sperm whale's equivalent of an oyster's pearl. The whales secrete a waxy substance that protects their insides from hard squid beaks. Usually, they get rid of this slippery mass quickly in their faeces, but a small proportion of sperm whales naturally have a constriction in their intestines and the congealed beaks build up into a large, solid mass. Ambergris is still an expensive perfumery ingredient. In many countries, it's illegal to own and trade it, but occasionally million-dollar lumps wash up on beaches.

When a sperm whale's digestive system is working normally, it performs a silent service to the planet. While hunting in the deep, most of their bodily functions shut down to save oxygen for the muscles and brain. Back at the surface, the whale breathes and defecates, releasing iron-rich liquid faeces that act as a perfect fertilizer and trigger blooms of plankton, the tiny algae that harness carbon from the atmosphere. Before commercial whaling, there were enough sperm whales swimming in the ocean around Antarctica to remove two million tonnes of carbon from the atmosphere every year.

People have found uses for another sperm-whale body part. To pass the downtime on whaling voyages that lasted for years, sailors practised the art of scrimshaw, using needles to scratch pictures into whalebone and sperm-whale teeth. Still today, in Fiji, when men ask their sweetheart's parents for permission to marry, some will make a traditional offering of sperm-whale teeth strung on braided cords. Some families have a stash of heirloom teeth – known as *tabua* – ready for such occasions. Fijians have never hunted whales, but they collected teeth from beached animals and in the past traded them from the neighbouring island, Tonga. Now the international trade in any sperm-whale body parts is prohibited. The limited supply of genuine teeth (there are fakes on the market) can sell for as much as a thousand dollars apiece, and young men often save up for years to buy enough *tabua* before they can get engaged.

When commercial hunting began in the North Pacific, sperm whales were not too difficult to catch. They often tried to defend themselves by crowding together at the surface. This was an effective strategy against their only other natural predators – orcas – but made them more vulnerable to humans. However, the old logbooks of whaling ships have revealed that within two years the whalers' success rate dropped by 58 per cent. Scientists think the sperm whales learned how to escape upwind, and even to attack whaling boats. What's more, the whales probably taught each other how to protect themselves. Sperm whales live in highly social, matrilineal families. It's possible that families with experience of whalers showed more naive whales what to do when they were attacked. Even though sperm whales got wise to American whalers, still a huge number were killed, and the hunt ramped up as diesel-powered ships and explosive harpoons were introduced. In the twentieth century alone, whalers killed more than 760,000 sperm whales. It's thought around 360,000 are alive today.

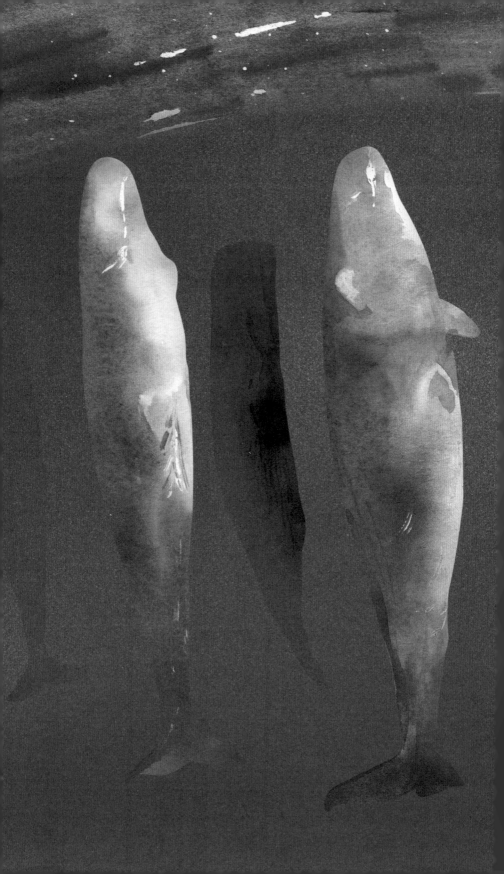

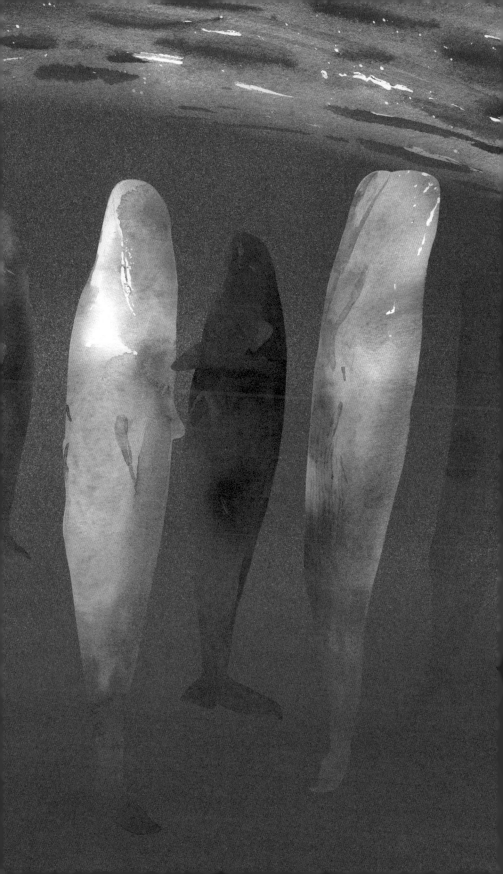

Lanternfish

Myctophidae

The most abundant fish in the ocean, and arguably the most important, are ones that few people ever see. Lanternfish spend their daytimes hidden down in the shadowy waters of the twilight zone, hundreds of metres underwater. There are around 250 species of these silvery, thumb-sized fish that look a bit like sardines with big eyes, blunt snouts and glowing dots of blue lights flashing across their bodies. A global headcount on these superabundant fish would be practically impossible, but estimates suggest there are hundreds of trillions, possibly thousands of trillions of them alive today. This not only makes them the most numerous fish, but also means there are more of them than of any other vertebrate on Earth (compare that to approximately 24 billion domestic chickens, for example).

The lanternfish family has been known of since the nineteenth century, but it wasn't until the 1950s that people started wondering just how many of them there might be. Scientists and naval officers were using newly developed sonar devices to measure the ocean's depth and to detect animals and submarines a long way underwater. They were puzzled when their sonar readouts showed what appeared to be a solid sea floor that moved towards the surface at night, then sank back to greater depths at dawn. Up and down it went, like clockwork. It turns out the beams of sonar were bouncing off the reflective swim bladders of trillions of lanternfish. They shoal in huge, dense layers, spread over hundreds of square kilometres. At night they all migrate towards the surface to feed on plankton under cover of darkness. Then, as the sun rises, they journey back into the deep. It's the biggest animal migration on the planet and it happens every day, all around the world.

In common with many animals that inhabit the open waters of the deep sea, lanternfish use their glowing lights to hide themselves when there's nothing to hide behind. Known as counter-illumination, the idea is that the blue light they produce across their bellies prevents them from showing up as dark silhouettes when seen from below. Predators below might otherwise easily make out the fish-shaped shadow and lunge for the kill. Lanternfish have additional rows of lights dotted along their flanks. These are probably used for communication, perhaps as a way for the fish to coordinate their movements in those enormous shoals so they don't bump into each other. The pattern of lights also differs between species, suggesting they play some role in lanternfish identifying each other, perhaps in a kind of twinkling courtship.

These prolific fish are critical in the ocean's ecosystems, partly because many animals eat them, including tuna, sharks, octopuses, squid, seals, penguins, seabirds, dolphins and whales. What's more, their daily migrations are vital for the climate. Lanternfish help to keep the Earth cool. Feeding at night at the surface, they consume enormous amounts of organic matter in the form of plankton, which they then actively pull down into the deep sea each night. In doing so, lanternfish – and other migrating animals such as siphonophores and jellyfish – draw millions of tonnes of carbon into the deep every year, releasing it in their droppings and as they breathe out. Once dissolved carbon is injected in this way into deep waters, it can stay locked away from the atmosphere for millennia.

For now, the tremendous biomass of lanternfish across the ocean remains largely untouched, but some people find them too tempting to leave alone. Several experimental enterprises are trying to work out if it's possible to turn a profit fishing lanternfish. They're too oily and full of bones for human consumption, but could be mashed into fish meal and oils to feed salmon in fish farms. If lanternfish fisheries scaled up, they would risk upsetting the balance of the ocean and making climate change even worse.

Spiny Dogfish

Squalus acanthias

Many people have eaten sharks without realizing it. You won't see dogfish on the menu, but rock salmon has been a staple in British fish-and-chip shops for decades. This name-switching was part of a rebranding exercise aimed at persuading more people to eat the sharks that industrial trawlers were beginning to catch a lot of. Spiny dogfish are also sold as huss. Around the world, various other shark species have been marketed under different, non-sharky names, including flake in Australia, whitefish and steakfish in the United States, *saumonette* in France and *vitello di mare*, 'veal of the sea', in Italy.

Fishing for spiny dogfish has been so intense in the Atlantic that the population has declined by more than 95 per cent since 1905, and the species is listed as vulnerable to extinction. This partly comes down to the fact that it takes male dogfish 10 years and females 20 years to reach maturity, which is distinctly old for a fish. And once the females are finally old enough to start breeding, they are pregnant for two years – as long as an elephant – before giving birth to a relatively meagre litter of about six or seven pups. It means the species is not well suited to high levels of fishing and populations take a long time to recover.

There are more than 100 species in the dogfish or dog shark family (Squalidae) worldwide. There are also about 150 species of catshark (Scyliorhinidae) swimming through the seas, with elongated, cat-like eyes, although confusingly some of them are known as dogfish. However, the two groups are easily distinguished by the way they reproduce. Dogfish give birth to live young, and catsharks lay eggs.

Electric Torpedo Ray

Torpedo torpedo

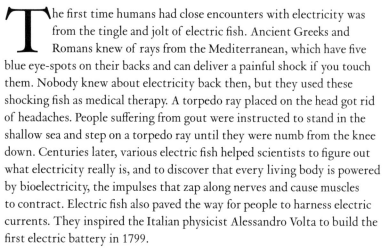

The first time humans had close encounters with electricity was from the tingle and jolt of electric fish. Ancient Greeks and Romans knew of rays from the Mediterranean, which have five blue eye-spots on their backs and can deliver a painful shock if you touch them. Nobody knew about electricity back then, but they used these shocking fish as medical therapy. A torpedo ray placed on the head got rid of headaches. People suffering from gout were instructed to stand in the shallow sea and step on a torpedo ray until they were numb from the knee down. Centuries later, various electric fish helped scientists to figure out what electricity really is, and to discover that every living body is powered by bioelectricity, the impulses that zap along nerves and cause muscles to contract. Electric fish also paved the way for people to harness electric currents. They inspired the Italian physicist Alessandro Volta to build the first electric battery in 1799.

Electric rays hunt at night. They hide in the seabed and stun prey with a 220-volt electric shock generated by a pair of kidney-shaped organs on either side of their body, evolved from modified muscles in their gills. These organs are packed with cells, called electrocytes, that have lost their ability to contract and instead push charged ions across the cell membranes. This builds up a stored electric charge like a battery, which can then be released all at once.

As well as torpedoes, there are dozens of electric rays, including numbfishes (Narcinidae), sleeper rays (Narkinae) and coffin rays (Hypnidae). There are also electric bony fish, such as the northern stargazers (*Astroscopus guttatus*) that live along the Atlantic coast of the United States, from North Carolina to New York, and generate weak electric shocks between their skyward-facing eyes. Living in fresh waters there are electric catfish, electric elephantfish and many different knifefish, including the infamous electric eels, which are not in fact eels (Malapteruridae, Mormyridae and *Electrophorus electricus*). In all, the ability to emit an electric charge has evolved on at least six separate occasions among distantly related fish, all of which ignore the health-and-safety warning never to mix electricity and water.

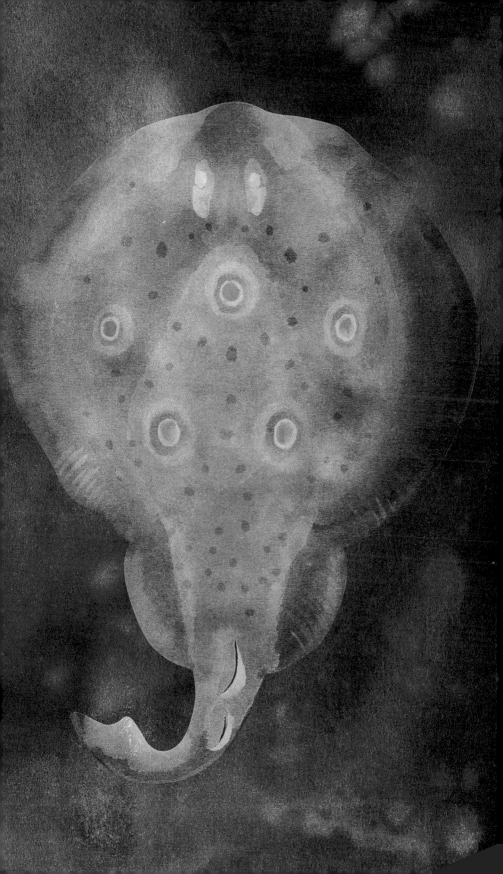

Noble Pen Shell

Pinna nobilis

For thousands of years people have told stories about a fine fabric called sea silk. In ancient Egypt, kings were mummified and buried wrapped in sea-silk cloaks. Roman emperors wore robes trimmed with sea silk. Some have said that when the mythological Greek hero Jason went on his quest for a golden fleece, he and his army of Argonauts were in fact searching for an item made of sea silk. Third-century Chinese traders claimed that sea silk came from water sheep, which climbed out of the sea, rubbed themselves against rocks and left behind golden tufts that people gathered and spun into thread. Unsurprisingly, many of these stories turned out to be untrue, in part owing to a historical spelling mistake. However, more believable stories did begin to emerge about a genuine cloth called sea silk. It was made from the golden beards of giant sea shells – that much at least is true.

The noble pen shell is the biggest species in its family, also known as fan mussels. Their shells can stand a metre (3 ft) tall from seagrass meadows with the pointed end poked into the seabed, anchored with a net of sticky threads. Other bivalves make similar clumps of threads; this is the beard that chefs pull off blue mussels (*Mytilus edulis*) while preparing a bowl of moules marinière. Pen shells make these threads by secreting a liquid protein along a groove in their muscly foot, and waiting a moment while it sets hard. A full beard contains about 1,000 threads, each one up to 20 centimetres (8 in) long. And these can indeed be extracted and spun into threads then woven into a woolly fabric known as sea silk.

The oldest confirmed fragment of sea silk, found in Budapest, dates from the fourth century (it's possible to identify the threads because under a microscope they're egg-shaped in cross section). A close-fitting cap made of sea silk was found in Paris, dating from the fourteenth century. Many more sea-silk objects, including gloves and scarves, come from the eighteenth and nineteenth centuries, when they were popular across Europe in cabinets of curiosities. In 1804 Horatio Nelson gave his lover Emma Hamilton a pair of sea-silk gloves from Sardinia. Italy was traditionally the centre for sea-silk weaving, and today Sardinia is the only place where it's made. The practice is kept alive by a few women who know how to spin the beards into golden threads that look like fine wool. But they can't go fishing to get more beards to work with because pen shells are now a protected species. They must make do with collections of old beards passed down to them from their grandmothers.

The beardy threads of bivalves are also known as byssus, which is where the earlier confusion over sea silk came from. The word byssus, spelled in various ways, appears in ancient languages, including Hebrew, Greek and Latin. Depending on the precise spelling, it could refer to the threads of a pen shell, as Aristotle used it in his book *Historia animalium* (The History of Animals). (The word comes from the ancient Greek for depth, and also gave us the word abyss.) Another ancient spelling of byssus refers to any fine cloth made of cotton, silk or linen, not specifically sea silk. Amid various spelling mistakes and mistranslations, scholars got into the habit of assuming that any old texts mentioning byssus were referring to sea silk – hence the popular association of this oceanic thread with everything from golden fleeces to Egyptian mummies.

Genuine sea silk has always been rare, but the pen shells have become an even rarer sight since the Mediterranean was hit by a silent killer. Since 2016 a deadly disease has been wiping out pen shells in Spain and Italy. Conservationists are monitoring the situation anxiously, and fear the extinction of the species.

Spiny Oyster

Spondylus spp.

I t's tricky to spot a spiny oyster in the wild. Their prongs encourage seaweeds and sponges to grow all over them, giving them excellent camouflage on rocky reefs and coral reefs. Find an empty one and you'll see that underneath all those living adornments the shell can be deep orange, purple, blood-red or pure, gleaming white. It is perhaps these colours that have attracted people for millennia.

During the Neolithic period, people collected spiny oysters from the Aegean Sea, carved them into jewellery and ornaments, and traded them far across Europe. In the Bulgarian city of Varna, an ancient necropolis was found dating back 6,500 years, containing hundreds of graves including that of the leader of this ancient community, who was buried with a hoard of gold jewellery. Among his finery was a bangle around his bicep that was carved from a single spiny-oyster shell. For some mysterious reason it had been deliberately broken in two, then fixed with ornamental gold plate. Other ancient objects made of spiny-oyster shells from the Mediterranean have been found in ancient graves across Ukraine, the Balkans, Hungary, Poland, Germany and France. They include beads, buttons, pendants and belt buckles. The shells became increasingly popular into the Copper Age, then about 3,000 years ago they vanished from the archaeological record.

Thousands of miles away, trades emerged in other species of spiny oyster. Archaeologists have traced the shells, as well as images and ceramic replicas of them, throughout the Aztec, Mayan and Incan civilizations. There, as in Europe, the shells were carved into beads and jewellery. Whole spiny oysters were left in graves, such as the 200 huge shells found in a tomb in Peru, built by the Lambayeque culture around 1000 CE.

Spiny oysters are not in fact oysters at all, but more closely related to scallops. Since ancient times people have eaten them, including, perhaps, during shamanistic rituals. Archaeologists have speculated that priests in ancient Andean cultures deliberately ate contaminated oysters for their psychotropic effects. Eat an oyster during a red tide, when the sea blooms with toxic plankton, and you will probably catch paralytic shellfish poisoning, which makes you feel numb, giddy and sometimes as if you are flying.

Sponge

Porifera

Long before plastics were invented, people gathered sponges from the sea and put them to various uses. Since antiquity, people have used sea sponges for bathing and scrubbing their backs. Roman centurions stuffed sponges into their helmets as padding. Art historians can work out the age of a piece of pottery based on the type of sponge used to apply the glaze. In the late nineteenth century sponges played a clandestine role in women's reproductive freedom. Birth control was still highly controversial, and women used sea sponges soaked in antiseptic chemicals as a form of contraception.

Sponges may look like plants or giant fungi but they're animals; in fact, they were among the earliest to evolve hundreds of millions of years ago (scientists are still divided over which were the very oldest animals). Present-day sponges spend their lives filtering water through their porous bodies. They grow in a huge range of shapes and colours; there are giant barrels big enough to curl up inside, tall candelabras and chimneys, and some look like rainbow slime smeared across coral reefs. Time-lapse cameras recently showed deep-sea sponges perform slow-motion sneezes that take weeks to complete.

People aren't the only animals to use sponges. Dolphins in Australia go hunting with sponges on their snouts, presumably as protection while they rummage through the seabed. It's a new trick that dolphins teach each other, although curiously only the females.

For a long time Greece was the world's sponge-diving capital. Originally, divers held their breath and sank down holding on to heavy stones. But by the turn of the twentieth century hard-helmet diving suits had transformed the trade, and divers could go deeper and stay down longer than ever before.

Sponges also became big business in Florida. At the height of the fishery, around 200,000 tonnes of sponges were taken each year from the Florida Keys. Various sponges were targeted, the most valuable being 'wool' and 'velvet' varieties, which don't contain sharp silica spicules as many sponges do, but are mostly composed of elastic fibres called spongin.

Trouble lay ahead for the Florida sponge industry. As sponge beds were depleted, divers ventured further from shore and deeper underwater to find more. Then, in 1938, a deadly disease swept through the Caribbean, killing off sponges. The industry collapsed and sponge fishers were left destitute. The fishery itself may have accelerated its own demise. Fishers mistakenly thought that squeezing out the living part of the sponge, the so-called gurry, released seeds into the sea from which more sponges would grow. More likely, this practice helped to spread infectious microbes that the sponges had picked up from the sea. They aren't called sponges for nothing: tropical sponges can filter 200,000 times their own volume within 24 hours, filtering 90 per cent of the bacteria present. As sponge populations were over-fished around Florida, they no longer performed their ecological service of filtering huge quantities of bacteria from the sea. And there's evidence that as bacteria become abundant, they're more likely to switch from being relatively harmless to downright virulent.

Today, interest in sponges has turned from their physical uses to their chemical potential. Scientists are discovering masses of potent compounds inside them. Already, numerous medicines exist that were inspired by sponge-derived chemicals, including the anti-leukaemia drug cytarabine and the breast-cancer chemotherapy drug eribulin. Malaria treatments, new antibiotics capable of killing superbugs, and many other medicines are in the pipeline. Searching the seas for potentially useful chemicals has become much faster and more eco-friendly. It's no longer necessary to trawl up tonnes of sponges to extract chemicals. Now scientists carefully take small snippets from living sponges to test in labs. Any compounds of interest are then synthesized – and definitely not harvested from the wild. Of growing interest are sponges from the deep sea, where there's an untapped treasure trove of unknown species and a huge variety of complex chemicals to explore.

Argonaut

Argonauta spp.

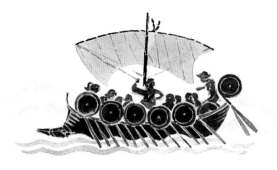

D rifting through the seas are small octopuses hiding inside delicate, gleaming shells. The ancient Greek philosopher Aristotle wrote about them. He described how the octopus uses the shell as a little boat, raising its sails into the air, in the form of two arms with wide webs at the end that catch the breeze and propel the tiny sailor and their vessel across the waves. It's a story that has been retold often over the centuries, and meanwhile the true identity of these octopuses and their shells remained a topic of hot debate among naturalists. For a long time many people thought these were two separate species. Argonauts – named after the Greek heroes who sailed with Jason on his ship the *Argo* – were the mysterious animals that made the shells. But no one ever saw a live specimen because, so it was thought, octopuses attack the argonauts, eat them, steal their shells then sail off over the horizon. An alternative view held that octopus and argonaut were one and the same animal.

The puzzle of the argonauts was solved in the 1830s by Jeanne Villepreux-Power, a French scientist who was something of a Gerald Durrell of her time. Originally a seamstress, she married a wealthy merchant and moved to Sicily, where she set about studying the island's wildlife. She brought animals into her home to study, and invented a glass-sided box, which she filled with seawater and sea creatures, including argonaut shells with octopuses inside, caught by local fishermen. Using her pioneering aquarium tank, she conducted a series of observations and experiments to find out the truth about argonauts. She noted that the little octopuses easily came all the way out of their shells, unlike snails and clams, which are permanently fixed inside theirs. When she took away the octopuses' shells they didn't grow new ones. But they did mend cracks, rubbing their shells with the silvery webs on the end of their arms. And when she chipped off chunks of their shells, the octopuses searched through the pieces at the bottom of the aquarium tank, finding the one that fitted the hole and gluing it back in place.

A final piece of evidence came from the eggs Villepreux-Power found inside the shells. When new hatchlings reached the size of a fingernail, she saw the tiny octopuses growing shells. Finally, she had proof that these animals were not shell-stealing pirates, but the argonauts themselves – the shell-making octopuses.

Millions of years ago the ancestors of octopuses stopped making shells. Then the group that evolved into argonauts started doing it again, only in a completely different way. Instead of secreting shell material from the soft body tissue called the mantle (the pink part of a mussel in a bowl of moules marinière), argonauts use those two special, webbed arms.

There are four known species of argonaut in the world's seas. Sometimes they ride on jellyfish, presumably using the stingers as protection. They may also chew through the jelly's body and steal particles of their food. Another name for argonauts is the paper nautilus because their shells look somewhat like chambered nautiluses. They aren't closely related, but it's a case of convergent evolution, of two groups finding a similar solution to the same challenge, in this case that of making a streamlined shell.

It's only female argonauts that make shells; the males are tiny and rarely seen. Their contribution to life is to approach a female and give her one of their arms. Back in Villepreux-Power's time, those dismembered arms were mistaken for parasitic worms. The specialized, sperm-laden limb, known as the hectocotylus, is a common octopus feature. Each female argonaut carries around several at a time until she needs them to fertilize her eggs. Then her shell becomes a mobile brood chamber, somewhere to rear her young until they're ready to start life on their own.

Octocoral

Octocorallia

Peer closely at the tiny, flower-like polyp of a coral and count the 'petals' (in fact they are tentacles). If there are eight, it is an octocoral. An older name for many of them is gorgonian, after the terrifying snake-haired Gorgons of Greek mythology, who turned into stone anyone who looked at them. In Ovid's *Metamorphosis*, Perseus cut off the head of Medusa, queen Gorgon, and laid it on a bed of seaweed, which turned to stone and, in some tellings, the precious red octocoral, *Corallium rubrum*.

For thousands of years people have admired, cherished and imbued with great power the fiery skeleton of red coral. The Romans traded red coral beads and ornaments with China and India, exchanging them for silk, pearls and black pepper. Red coral became a cure-all in cultures worldwide. It was thought to protect its wearer against ills and spells, improve fertility, ensure good crops and guard against storms. And, in common with so many magical oceanic products – from fossilized shark teeth to narwhal horns – red coral was believed to be a detector of and antidote for poison. In medieval Italy, coral was a protective amulet for children, and the infant Jesus is sometimes portrayed in paintings wearing a red coral branch as a pendant. In Edo-period Japan, red coral was worn by ladies as ornaments in their hair and carved into miniature sculpted *netsuke*.

Italy has long been the centre of the trade in red coral. At first, free-divers would hold their breath, swim down and snap off the tree-like colonies from the seabed. As demand grew and shallow coral beds were depleted, devices were invented to bring up corals from deeper underwater. The *ignegno* was a cross made of two wooden beams, laden with weights and nets to entangle coral colonies. A bigger, heavier device was the *barra italiana*, a 6-metre (20-ft), 1-tonne metal tube hung with long metal chains that dragged across the seabed, smashing delicate coral habitats. The arrival of helmet diving suits and eventually scuba equipment opened yet more opportunities for gathering red coral. Fishing for *C. rubrum* spread to other parts of the Mediterranean, and other species were found in the North Pacific in various shades of crimson, blood-red and peachy pink. Since the 1970s, precious corals have been dragged up by deep-sea trawlers from the sides of underwater mountains called seamounts.

Following centuries of exploitation, it's no wonder slow-growing colonies of red corals have been hit hard, and in many places they remain badly depleted. Various countries have introduced efforts to control the trade, but it's not clear whether these measures are enough to ensure a sustainable supply. Some jewellers, including Tiffany & Co., refuse to use new red coral at all.

The ocean contains thousands of other octocoral species, about three quarters of which live in the deep sea. There are bubblegum corals (Paragorgiidae), bamboo corals (Isididae) and sea pens (Pennatulacea), which look like feathery plumes a metre (3 ft) or more tall. Corals in the genus *Iridogorgia* look like giant shining bottlebrushes. On seamounts, octocorals grow alongside other corals and sponges, which together form rich forests where all sorts of animals live. Perched among the branches are squat lobsters, sea anemones and brittlestars. Deep-sea cat sharks lay their egg cases on corals like Christmas tree decorations.

Despite living in the dark deep, octocorals grow in rainbow colours and can be as eye-catching as coral reefs in shallow seas. The bright pigments probably serve a purpose other than being seen. Maybe they taste bad and deter coral-munching predators, which is an important strategy for long-lived corals. Bamboo corals can live for centuries, and relatives of octocorals can survive for millennia. Gold coral colonies (*Savalia* spp.) can grow for 2,700 years. And there are shrub-like colonies of black corals (*Leiopathes* spp.) alive today that started growing 4,200 years ago, around the time the ancient Egyptians were building their great pyramids.

Other varieties, known as stony corals (in the order Scleractinia), grow branching skeletons made of limestone and form enormous thickets in the deep sea, creating habitat for thousands of other species. In 1998 scientists discovered a huge field of deep-sea corals off the northwest coast of Scotland and named them the Darwin Mounds. In the Mediterranean and off the coast of Africa, scientists have discovered stony coral colonies that have been growing in the same place for 50,000 years. In comparison, the Great Barrier Reef has been growing for only around 8,000 years.

Common Octopus

Octopus vulgaris

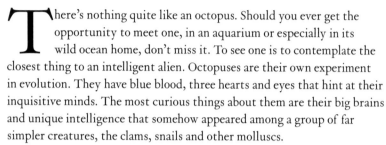

There's nothing quite like an octopus. Should you ever get the opportunity to meet one, in an aquarium or especially in its wild ocean home, don't miss it. To see one is to contemplate the closest thing to an intelligent alien. Octopuses are their own experiment in evolution. They have blue blood, three hearts and eyes that hint at their inquisitive minds. The most curious things about them are their big brains and unique intelligence that somehow appeared among a group of far simpler creatures, the clams, snails and other molluscs.

People are learning more all the time about octopuses' complex lives. Recently, scientists noticed that while they sleep, common octopuses change the colour and texture of their skin. Perhaps they're dreaming. Aquarium keepers tell stories of the playful octopuses with personalities: the ones that take against particular people and squirt water at them every time they walk by; the Houdinis that learn to escape by blocking the water outflow in their tanks and flooding the room; the ones that show how empty medicine bottles are childproof but certainly not octopus-proof.

No one yet knows for sure how octopuses evolved their unusual brainpower. Other molluscs, such as nudibranchs, have a few tens of thousands of neurons. Octopuses have half a billion. Around half of those are clustered in a doughnut-shaped ring in their heads, and the rest are in their arms. It's a completely different arrangement from that of humans and other vertebrates, which keep most of their neurons in their brains.

One theory of octopus evolution lays out a series of possible steps. First their ancestors lost their external shells, allowing them to become agile and swift predators. To control their wobbly bodies, octopus ancestors evolved large nervous systems. How else would they keep those eight unruly arms in order? Subsequently, they co-opted their nerves to develop complex behaviour and intelligence, necessary traits for surviving in a world where many animals want to eat soft, shell-less octopuses.

Roughly 300 octopus species live all around the ocean, from coastal tide pools to deep-sea hydrothermal vents, and they get up to all sorts of tricks. Mimic octopuses (*Thaumoctopus mimicus*) pretend to be dangerous by impersonating various other animals, from sea snakes to poisonous flatfish. Blue-ringed octopuses (*Hapalochlaena* spp.) really are deadly. Dumbo octopuses (*Grimpoteuthis* spp.) fly through the deep, flapping their ear-like fins. Blanket octopuses (*Tremoctopus* spp.) tear off the stinging tentacles of siphonophores to use as weapons.

Long before people started keeping and studying octopuses, these creatures were well known and even revered. Octopuses appear on Minoan and Mycenaean Bronze Age pottery that celebrated and worshipped the sea. Terracotta coffins called larnakes were decorated with images of octopuses, perhaps as symbols of regeneration after death – octopuses can regrow a lost arm.

More recently, we've come a long way in our attitudes to octopuses. In the 1960s octopus wrestling was a popular television event in America, as people dived down to yank giant Pacific octopuses (*Enteroctopus dofleini*) from their seabed hideaways. Nowadays viewers are absorbed by more compassionate portrayals of octopuses, and huge audiences tune into documentaries such as the enchanting film *My Octopus Teacher* (2020), which follows the life of a common octopus in False Bay, South Africa.

Octopuses are gaining wider recognition as animals that need careful treatment and respect. In 2021 lawmakers in the United Kingdom added octopuses, cuttlefish and squid (all types of cephalopod mollusc) to the official list of sentient beings – animals that can experience pleasure and joy, as well as pain and distress. Cephalopods, plus lobsters and crabs, are the first invertebrates to be included in the Animal Welfare (Sentience) Bill, which will protect them from unnecessary suffering. And yet, at around the same time, plans were announced for the world's first octopus farm. A Spanish company anticipates rearing 3,000 tonnes of common octopuses every year. Many scientists and animal welfare campaigners think mass-producing these intelligent, complex animals for human consumption would be unethical and should be banned before it starts.

People are looking to octopuses for more than just food. Engineers are imitating their nimble limbs to make soft robots with bionic tentacles and suction cups, that could assist in delicate surgery or be sent on missions to dangerous, far-flung places. Here on Earth, intelligent life has evolved at least twice – once among vertebrates, including us humans, and independently among octopuses. So maybe there are intelligent aliens elsewhere in the universe too.

Great White Shark

Carcharodon carcharias

Steven Spielberg's movie *Jaws* (1975) put great white sharks firmly in the public consciousness, and not for good reasons. Decades later the terror spawned by this fictional fish still convinces many people to be scared of shark-infested waters. There are occasional tragic encounters between humans and great whites, but even though other predators, such as bears in North America or crocodiles in Africa, cause more fatalities, still they're not as widely feared as sharks. As scientists learn more about the lives of great white sharks, they're seeing that these apex predators lead complex, thoughtful lives and are not simply mindless killing machines.

Satellite tracking devices have revealed that great white sharks go on long, purposeful journeys. No one knows for sure how sharks navigate, but it's possible the electrosensitive pores on their snouts allow them to detect weak electric currents generated by the Earth's magnetic field. In 2003 a shark that scientists named Nicole broke all records by swimming from South Africa to Australia and back again. In nine months Nicole swam 20,000 kilometres (12,400 miles), most likely in search of mating and feeding grounds. Each winter a huge congregation of great whites forms part way between Hawaii and Mexico. In this area, known as the White Shark Cafe, the sharks dive hundreds of metres into the twilight zone, possibly to hunt shoals of fish and squid.

To sustain themselves on long migrations, when they might not find many seals or sea lions to eat, great whites draw on energy from their enormous livers, which act like a camel's hump. A shark liver weighing half a tonne contains about 400 litres (700 pints) of oil that provides the equivalent in calorific terms of around 9,000 chocolate bars.

Long before there were sophisticated tracking devices to explore the lives of these creatures, people saw great white sharks only occasionally, when fishermen caught them. More familiar were triangular objects known as glossopetrae, tongue stones, which weren't at first associated with sharks. The Roman naturalist Pliny the Elder wrote that glossopetrae fell from the heavens during lunar eclipses. Other stories told of dragon or snake tongues being turned to stone. In the Middle Ages people believed glossopetrae were endowed with great power, and wore them as amulets or stitched into special pockets in their clothes. These mysterious stones were widely believed to be a cure for snake bites and an antidote to poison. Powdered glossopetrae were sold as remedies for epilepsy, fevers and bad breath. In 1666 the Danish anatomist Nicolas Steno dissected the head of a great white caught off the coast of Italy and was convinced that glossopetrae were in fact ancient fossilized shark teeth. He worked out that these triangular stones were the remains of sharks from a previous geological era, and in doing so he pioneered a whole new view of the Earth's ancient history.

Some of the biggest fossil shark teeth come from extinct megalodons. Given their teeth were up to three times bigger than great whites, it is likely megalodons may have grown to 16 or 18 metres (52–60 ft) long, almost the length of two London buses. Palaeontologists used to think the megalodon's closest living relatives were great white sharks, but now they've been put in a separate family of extinct sharks.

Great whites are members of the Lamnidae family, named after Lamnia, a child-eating monster of Greek mythology. Other living lamnid sharks are porbeagles, salmon sharks and both the longfin and shortfin makos, which have a reputation as the cheetahs of the ocean and can swim at up to 70 kilometres (45 miles) per hour. Some of the secrets to their immense speed are patches of tiny, flexible teeth-like denticles on their skin. Engineers worked out that mako sharks' wobbly denticles help to stop vortices forming in the water behind their gills and fins, reducing drag and improving their efficiency as they speed through the water.

Designers of swimwear have looked to sharks for inspiration to help humans move through the water faster. In 2000 Speedo released Fastskin, an ankle-to-wrist swimsuit covered in V-shaped ridges, designed to mimic shark denticles. And it seemed to work. At the Sydney Olympics, eight out of ten swimmers who won medals were wearing Fastskin suits. New, improved suits were developed and more records were smashed. Then, in 2012, an ichthyologist at Harvard University tested the suits and found that they don't actually reduce drag in the way shark denticles do. In fact, they work by trapping air bubbles and helping swimmers to float, reducing friction in the water. The International Swimming Federation has now banned full-length, shark-inspired suits.

MEDITERRANEAN

Remora/Shark Sucker

Echeneidae

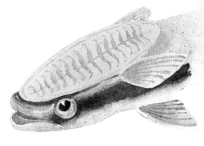

In 31 BCE, off the coast of Greece, the Roman general Mark Antony and the Queen of Egypt, Cleopatra, lost a naval battle that led to the end of the Roman Republic and the beginning of the Roman Empire. The victor, later known as Emperor Augustus, become the undisputed master of the Roman world. The Roman writer Pliny the Elder laid speculative blame for Antony and Cleopatra's defeat on fish. The ships in their fleets had been gripped and held back by shoals of *Echeneis*, the ship holders.

Stories of foot-long (30 cm) fish that latch on to ships' hulls and slow them down remained popular into medieval times. The ocean is home to eight species that are a good fit for these nautical troublemakers. Remoras do sometimes grab boats, but usually they prefer dolphins, turtles, whales, sharks and other big fish. In 2020 an underwater photographer snapped a picture of a whale shark swimming along with 20 remoras inside its open mouth. While they don't bring boats or sharks to a standstill, remoras do add hydrodynamic drag. Dolphins laden with remoras can be seen leaping from the water, perhaps trying to dislodge their hitchhikers.

Remoras look as though they've been trodden on by someone wearing a large wellington boot. The oval, ridged suction cup on their heads is formed at a young age from a modified dorsal fin. It allows them to save energy by holding on to bigger animals instead of swimming. When they're being carried along fast enough, remoras don't even need to breathe actively; they simply open their mouths and let the water flow over their gills.

There's a long history of fishermen using remoras as living fishhooks to help them hunt. Stories brought back from Christopher Columbus's second voyage to the Caribbean include fishermen tying strings around the tails of eel-shaped fish the Spanish called *reversus*. Fishers would let the fish swim off and fix themselves to the shells of turtles, then haul them in. Similar reports came from Zanzibar, South Africa and Madagascar in the nineteenth century.

Other non-suckered fish hang around sharks. Pilotfish are especially fond of oceanic whitetip sharks, often swimming ahead of them in their bow wave. Their name stems from ancient stories that tell of these fish leading sharks to find food or showing ships which way to go.

In a 2021 study, scientists gathered underwater footage posted on YouTube by scuba divers and saw dozens of instances of fish swimming up to sharks, including great whites, and rubbing up against their skin. It seems a risky strategy to approach a giant predator, rather than scarpering. But it does make sense for fish to use shark skin to exfoliate and rub off their own parasites, especially in open seas, where there are no cleaner wrasse nearby to do the job.

Portuguese Man o' War

Physalia physalis

I f you spy a pink balloon bobbing out at sea or washed up on a beach,
chances are you've found a Portuguese man o' war. Like a jellyfish – but
not quite – this is a close relative, a siphonophore. The ocean is full of
hundreds of siphonophore species, but most stay hidden beneath the waves.
It's only the Portuguese man o' war that has a pneumatic float keeping it
visible at the surface and catching the breeze as it sails across wide ocean
basins. It is said by some people that these floats resemble eighteenth-
century man-o'-war frigates, hence the creature's name. Sometimes great
armadas sweep on to coastlines and local authorities close beaches to save
swimmers from getting stung.

Siphonophores build their body like no other animals. They're made
up of colonies of clones, called zooids, all of which play a key role; some
catch food, some produce eggs or sperm, and some move and steer the
colony with rhythmic contractions of tiny, jellyfish-like bells.

With their delicate, gelatinous bodies, most siphonophores are
notoriously difficult to study. For a start, they fall apart in sampling nets.
But, using deep-diving robots, biologists are finding more siphonophores
and discovering how important they are for ocean ecosystems. They
grow in elaborate shapes, and some are huge. The biggest so far, around
30 metres (98 ft) long, was filmed off the coast of Western Australia
hanging in a giant spiral.

Siphonophores are hidden heroes of the climate. They join an immense
migration of animals that rise to the surface at night to feed, then sink at
sunrise, dragging billions of tonnes of carbon each year into the deep, where
it stays away from the atmosphere for millennia. But not the Portuguese
man o' war – they just stay floating.

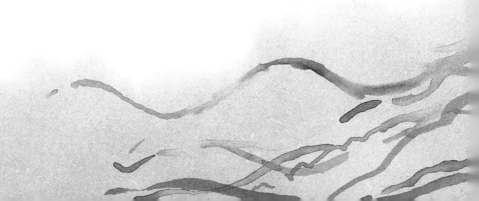

Scaly-Foot Snail

Chrysomallon squamiferum

S caly-foot snails are among the strange life forms that live in the deep sea on hydrothermal vents. They have a foot covered in scales and a shiny shell made of iron, two features that make them unique. No other snails have scaly feet – they're usually soft and squashy – and no animal is known to have iron-based body armour. The way these snails make theirs could prove to be very useful for people, too.

Hydrothermal vents, also known as black smokers, are some of the most extreme environments on Earth. They form miles beneath the surface, at crushing depths, and have scorching, toxic fluids pouring out of them. When the peculiar scaly snails were first found, in 2001, deep-sea biologists thought the scales and iron shell might somehow protect these creatures from their unpleasant surroundings. In fact, the snails' unusual features protect them from a threat that comes from within.

The snails get their food from colonies of bacteria living inside a special pouch in their throat. These bacteria harness energy from the chemicals emitted by the black smoker chimneys. It's thanks to the bacteria that life flourishes around black smokers, in total darkness, completely cut off from sunlight. For the snails, and many other animals living on vents, it's a symbiotic partnership. The bacteria get a safe place to live and a constant supply of the chemicals they need, while the snails get all the food they need from the bacteria living inside them.

But there is one problem. In the process of generating food from chemicals, including hydrogen sulphide, the bacteria also release sulphur, which happens to be poisonous to snails. To get rid of this toxin, the snails' scales are made up of thousands of tiny tubes that act like exhaust pipes. The sulphur passes along the pipes and, on reaching the surface, reacts with iron in the seawater, forming particles of iron compounds including iron pyrite, otherwise known as fool's gold. That's how the snails get their shining armour and how they survive with sulphur-making bacteria inside them.

Unlocking the scaly-foot snails' secret offers great promise for advances in manufacturing. Tiny particles of iron have many industrial applications, including solar panels and rechargeable batteries, but making them currently involves a costly, high-temperature process. Scaly-foot snails are showing that it's possible to make iron particles at much lower temperatures; they usually hang around the parts of vents that are about

15ºC (60ºF). What's more, they don't have to be alive to do it; the scales and the tiny pipes work by themselves. Engineers could create their own versions and possibly inspire a new generation of more efficient industrial manufacturing. And don't worry, there'll be no need for factories with row upon row of captive scaly-foot snails.

Bluestreak Cleaner Wrasse

Labroides dimidiatus

If you're ever tempted to believe the stories that fish have only a seven-second memory or are unable to feel pain or joy, just remember the cleaner wrasse. On coral reefs across the tropics, busy scenes unfold at cleaner wrasse territories. Other fish arrive and patiently wait their turn to have bloodsucking parasites nibbled from their skin. Every day a cleaner wrasse will tend to hundreds of clients and remember each one, tailoring its services accordingly. It's what keeps the cleaner in business and, crucially, keeps them alive.

At a cleaning station, everyone follows strict etiquette and an intricate choreography plays out. First the cleaner wrasse, operating alone or in pairs, advertise their services by performing dances, flicking their tails rhythmically from side to side. Then, as they begin cleaning, their client holds perfectly still in a trance-like state. Many visiting fish are predators that could easily snack on the little cigar-sized wrasse once they've finished their cleaning duties, but a truce is struck and nobody gets eaten. Cleaner wrasse swim bravely into the gaping mouths of moray eels, groupers and other sharp-toothed hunters. It's like a lion tamer not just putting their head into a lion's jaws but climbing right inside. For those clients, cleaner wrasse are always on their best behaviour, especially for predators that haven't eaten in a while, which somehow the wrasse can sense. When their client is dangerous or hungry, cleaner wrasse only ever pick off parasites, dead skin and nothing more.

But harmless herbivores, such as rabbitfish and surgeonfish, don't always get such good treatment. Occasionally, the cleaner wrasse will cheat these clients and take a bite of living skin. They do this to get a mouthful of the slime that covers a fish's skin, and which helps prevent UV damage in these sun-soaked tropical waters. Fish don't make sunscreen themselves but obtain it in their diets, hence the cleaner wrasse sometimes taking a deeper bite – but they always make amends afterwards by rubbing and smoothing the client with an all-over fin massage. It's obvious that the client fish enjoy this physical contact as their eyes roll back in their heads and they seem to fall into a blissful trance. Scientists have measured stress hormones dropping in fishes' blood after a good rubbing. It's probably why fish keep visiting cleaning stations, sometimes hundreds of times a day, not because they're filthy with parasites but just because it feels good.

Cleaner wrasse also learn which fish have small territories and have no other cleaning stations within reach. Those ones may swim off in a huff when they get bitten, but the wrasse knows they will be back because they have no other choice.

As well as their impressive long-term memories and ability to sense the motivation of other fish, cleaner wrasse show other hints of advanced cognitive abilities. It's possible they are self-aware. In 2019 scientists in Germany published a study in which they kept ten cleaner wrasse in individual aquariums fitted out with a mirror. Initially, the fish darted at their reflections, mistaking themselves for an unwanted intruder. A day later they calmed down and started checking themselves out in the mirror. Next, scientists put a blob of coloured gel on each fish's head, and nine out of ten of them gazed at their reflection, perhaps noticing that their appearance had changed. Some rubbed their heads against the tank as if trying to dislodge the coloured dot. The wrasse did neither of these things when they were given a colourless dot.

The study was controversial, and not everyone agrees that it offers proof of self-awareness in cleaner wrasse, even though similar tests passed muster for dolphins, chimpanzees, crows and elephants. It seems fish may have to go to greater lengths to show they are not as dumb as many people think they are.

West Indian Ocean Coelacanth

Latimeria chalumnae

U ntil less than a century ago, scientists assumed coelacanths were
long gone. The only signs of these fish were fossilized remains
lodged deep in rocks dating as far back as the Devonian period,
about 400 million years ago. At least 100 species of coelacanth swam
through the ancient oceans, but only until the end of the Cretaceous.
Nobody has ever unearthed coelacanth fossils younger than 66 million
years old, and that seemed to suggest that this particular branch of the fish
family tree didn't survive the cataclysmic mass extinction that wiped out
the dinosaurs. But then, in 1938, fishers off the coast of South Africa made a
remarkable discovery.

When trawler captain Hendrik Goosen hauled up his net, he saw that
he had caught a fish unlike anything he'd seen before. It was 2 metres (6½
ft) long, royal blue, with an unusual three-part tail, and at the base of each
fin was a distinctive fleshy lobe. Goosen put the strange fish aside to show
to a local museum curator, Marjorie Courtenay-Latimer, who would often
come to search through his nets for interesting specimens. This fish was
something totally different, and Courtenay-Latimer couldn't find it in any
fish guidebooks. A while later the fish biologist J.L.B. Smith of Rhodes
University came to see the stuffed specimen and immediately identified
it as a coelacanth. It was the ichthyological equivalent of laying eyes on
a recently deceased *Velociraptor*. Smith named the new genus of living
coelacanths *Latimeria*, after Courtenay-Latimer.

Aside from finding an animal whose lineage had been presumed
extinct, there were other reasons why the discovery of coelacanths was so
groundbreaking. Scientists wondered whether ancestors of these fleshy-
finned fish gave rise to the first four-legged vertebrates that crawled out
of the sea on to land, leading to all the reptiles, amphibians, birds and
mammals. Recent genetic studies have, however, shown that it was more
likely lungfish, relatives of coelacanths, that were closest to the group of
ancient fish that made a break for land.

Since the first discovery of modern coelacanths off South Africa,
they've been found living off the Comoros islands, Kenya, Tanzania,
Mozambique and Madagascar. They inhabit the twilight zone, hundreds of
metres underwater, often huddled inside rocky caves, where they drift about
at night hunting for fish and squid. Their deep, shy nature is probably one

reason why they stayed hidden from Western science for so long. In 1997 the marine biologist Mark Erdmann spotted a second species, the Sulawesi coelacanth, *L. menadoensis*, in an Indonesian fish market.

Coelacanths have been labelled 'living fossils' because over millions of years their appearance didn't seem to have changed a great deal. But it's an undeserved reputation. In fact, coelacanths are not stuck in evolutionary stasis. Plenty has been changing at a genetic level, and over the last 10 million years coelacanths have gained more than 60 new genes thanks to a type of 'selfish gene' that jumps between species.

Nevertheless, the idea that coelacanths are ancient survivors has captured people's imaginations, and some even think eating them could lead to a longer life. Fortunately, these fish smell and taste terrible and have a strong laxative effect, so commercial coelacanth fisheries have never got going. But coelacanths are caught accidentally in shark fishing nets, which is why the West Indian Ocean species is now considered critically endangered.

Much of the unusual biology of coelacanths puts them at grave risk. They seem to be naturally rare, and only a few hundred are alive today. Females are pregnant for a record-breaking five years before giving birth to live pups. Recently scientists worked out that adults don't mature until they're at least 40 years old, and they can live for nearly a century. Coelacanths may not be living fossils, but they do live for a very long time – given the chance.

Giant Oceanic Manta Ray

Mobula birostris

To meet a giant oceanic manta ray is an enthralling experience. Their triangular wings can stretch to 7 metres (23 ft) across, and they weigh up to 3 tonnes. And these are giants that will do you absolutely no harm, except perhaps give you a rash if they rub their rough skin over yours the wrong way (but really you shouldn't be getting that close). They are gentle filter-feeders, formidable only to minute plankton. They fly through the water with tremendous grace, and they have a knowing look in their eyes that hints at something thoughtful going on inside.

Manta rays have the biggest brain-to-body ratio of any fish. A recent study of captive mantas offered some insights into what their huge brains might mean for them. At an aquarium in the Bahamas, scientists lowered a giant mirror into a tank where two manta rays were living. The pair proceeded to show a lot of interest in their reflection, circling in front of the mirror and blowing bubbles (mantas don't breathe air, and so can't exhale, but air bubbles can get lodged in and released from their gills). The scientists think the mantas may have been performing a behaviour known as contingency checking. You and I do the same when we wave a hand to check it's our own reflection we're seeing in a distant window. *Is that me? Ah, yes it is.* Not everyone agrees, but it's possible the mantas knew they were looking at themselves in that mirror, in a similar way to the cleaner wrasse that paid particular attention in the mirror to coloured dots put on their heads (the mantas were not given coloured dots).

In the wild, mantas could conceivably see themselves reflected in the surface of the sea, perhaps as they return from deep dives. Reef mantas (*Mobula alfredi*) have been recorded diving down to 700 metres (2,300 ft), plunging into distinctly chilly waters. As with most fish, their body temperature varies depending on their surroundings, and for a manta the optimal temperature is in the tropical range of 20–26°C (68–79°F). To keep their big brains from freezing during their deep dives, mantas have dense bundles of blood vessels that act as a countercurrent heat exchanger. Rather than losing the heat through their gills to the surrounding water, the flow of blood redirects the warmth back towards their vital organs. Mantas essentially have built-in brain-warmers.

Mantas have another smart gadget inside their mouths, one that stops their gills from becoming clogged as they filter minute food from the water.

They swim around in their mouth-open stance, constantly feeding, but they never cough and they don't have a tongue to dislodge anything that gets stuck in their gills. Instead, they've evolved gills covered in tiny comb-like teeth precisely shaped to stir swirling vortices that whip food particles into their throats while simultaneously keeping the gills clean. The mantas' self-cleaning gills are inspiring engineers to copy their trick and make devices that could sieve tiny flecks of plastic from wastewater at processing plants.

Sadly, another use has been invented for the mantas' gills. A decade or so ago traders in traditional Chinese medicine started selling manta gills to treat everything from acne to chickenpox. It seems traders made up these therapies, since mantas don't appear in any traditional medicine texts. They may have switched to manta gills as sharks became over-fished and their fins harder to come by. Now tens of thousands of mantas, and their relatives the devil rays, are killed for their gills every year, including in Vietnam, Sri Lanka, India and Indonesia. In many places mantas are now strictly protected and conservation groups are working to reduce demand, partly by highlighting to consumers that the gills are contaminated with dangerous levels of toxins, including arsenic and cadmium, that the mantas accumulate while swimming through the seas.

Giant Clam

Tridacna gigas

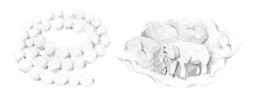

Myths of man-eating giant clams are just that. There's no reliable record of anyone actually being trapped and drowned by one of these huge bivalves. For one thing, they have hundreds of tiny eyes dotted across their soft mantle, the colourful tissue that peeps out from inside their open shells. While their eyesight is not very sharp, giant clams can sense light and dark, and when a shadow falls on them – such as that of a human diver – they quickly shut their shells, mostly likely before that person has a chance to reach in. What's more, giant clams are not predators waiting to spring their trap on unwitting prey; they're filter-feeders that strain small particles from the water. They also obtain energy from tiny algae, known as zooxanthellae, that live symbiotically within their tissues. A clam's iridescent colours come from specialized cells in the mantle, called iridocytes, that shine sunlight on to the algae to help them grow.

The true story of people and clams is much more the other way round. Human beings have been eating giant clams for millennia. One particular species, *Tridacna costata*, is now very rare across its range in the Red Sea. However, these clams used to be not only much more abundant but also much bigger – up to 20 times heavier than they are today. This clam shrinkage coincides with the time when early humans were probably migrating out of Africa, more than 100,000 years ago. We know these ancient hominids were seafood aficionados from the shucking tools they left behind around that time. By taking all the biggest, juiciest clams it's possible humans left a lasting impression on them.

Some people still like eating giant clams today, although the species is now widely protected. The favoured part is the large muscle that pulls the shells together. Giant clams are also hunted for their shells. *T. gigas* are the world's biggest bivalves, with shells that can be more than a metre (3 ft) across. There are also twelve somewhat smaller *Tridacna* species. Traditionally, the giant shells have been used as fonts in churches. A new threat is an illegal trade in giant clam shells for use a substitute for elephant ivory. Following the international crackdown on the trade in elephant tusks, traders have sought an alternative material and there has been a surge in giant clam trading. On the Chinese island of Hainan, artisans carve translucent giant clam shells into gleaming beads and intricate ornaments. In recent years dozens of illegal consignments of clam shells worth millions of dollars have been seized by customs. The biggest so far was in the Philippines in 2019, when officials confiscated 120,000 tonnes of shells. Conservationists are becoming increasingly concerned about the impact of the trade on clams and their coral-reef homes.

Tiger Shark

Galeocerdo cuvier

Tiger sharks are some of the biggest apex predators in the ocean, similar in size to great white sharks and commonly growing to 5 metres (16 ft) long. They're named for the stripes that are most prominent in the young sharks, and they roam warm and tropical coasts, where they have a profound influence on their environment – because a lot of animals are scared of them, as well they should be. Tiger sharks have a broad diet and attack all sorts of prey, from dolphins and dugongs to fish, sea snakes and sea turtles.

In Shark Bay in Western Australia is the world's biggest seagrass meadow. The bay is also home to thousands of grazing dugongs and plenty of tiger sharks that hunt them. When tiger sharks are around, dugongs behave cautiously. They spend less time with their heads down, chewing deep into the seagrass roots and ripping out whole plants. Instead they crop the tips of grass blades, which means they can eat while watching out for sharks. By scaring dugongs, tiger sharks are critical in keeping the whole seagrass ecosystem intact.

Without big sharks, seagrasses may struggle to survive climate change. In 2011 a huge heatwave hit Shark Bay and wiped out a quarter of all the seagrasses. The dugongs temporarily left the bay to look for other food. Scientists took the chance to study what would happen if there were no tiger sharks. Divers went out and impersonated dugongs, using trowels to dig up seagrasses just as the grazing mammals would do if there were no big sharks around to terrify them. They saw that the seagrasses struggled to recover because they were being disturbed too much by the divers' simulated grazing. Elsewhere, tiger sharks probably have more subtle ecological effects that are harder to detect, but it's likely they play a wider role in maintaining a healthy ocean.

Across the Pacific, Polynesian cultures have traditionally tapped into the tiger sharks' fearsome anatomy. Daggers, swords and spears have razor-sharp shark teeth fixed to them, each one individually drilled and tied on with string to a wooden base, sometimes entwined with strands of human hair. In Hawaii they were fashioned into paddle-shaped weapons for disembowelling an enemy. Teeth from various shark species appear on traditional weapons, but those of tiger sharks were a favourite for their unique doubled-serrated, sideways-pointing tip that is perfect for slashing flesh and bone. Their teeth allow tiger sharks to eat a wide range of prey, even chomping through the shells of sea turtles.

Teeth are all that remains of most ancient shark species, including at least six extinct species of tiger shark (today there's only one living member of the genus *Galeocerdo*). Shark skeletons, being made of soft cartilage and not hard bone, have not easily fossilized. Extremely rare fossil shark vertebrae recently found in Maryland have revealed evidence of ancient shark-on-shark battles. The fossils date back to between 23 and 2.5 million years ago, when megalodon sharks (*Otodus megalodon*) roamed the ocean. The backbones, one of which could be from an ancient tiger shark, are covered in shark bite marks. A few even have fossilized shark teeth still stuck in them, and one shows signs of healing, indicating that it was not a fatal attack.

In the ocean today, it's not unusual for sharks to hunt each other, even before they're born. Sand tiger sharks (*Carcharias taurus*) are distant relatives of tiger sharks. Females mate with several males and produce dozens of embryos inside a two-pronged uterus. While they're still inside their mother, the embryos hatch, and when they reach a finger's length in size they start attacking and eating each other until there are only two left. The twins keep growing, eating their mother's unfertilized eggs. Eventually they're born at around a metre (3 ft) long, big enough to avoid most other ocean predators, which gives them an excellent start in life.

Ocean Sunfish

Mola mola

If sunfish were truly to live up to their scientific name, *Mola mola* (from the Latin for 'millstone'), they wouldn't do at all well in water because they would sink. In fact, they do the opposite. These enormous grey, flat, rounded fish may look like giant grinding stones, but they float at the surface of the sea. Marine biologists used to think they did this to save energy and wait for jellyfish to drift past for them to eat. It could be that they lie there so that seabirds will come along and peck parasites from their skin. But with the help of electronic tags, an ichthyological equivalent of Fitbits, scientists from the University of Tokyo discovered not so long ago that these giants dive on long hunting forays into deep, cold waters, then return to the surface and bask in the sun to warm up. Their sunbathing behaviour is where their English common name comes from. In various other languages they're known as moonfish, including in French (*poisson lune*).

There's something distinctly stellar about sunfish. They begin life as spiky round balls drifting in the plankton. These young ones are clues that some of the sunfishes' close relatives are pufferfish. Soon, though, they lose their spines, gain weight and grow at tremendous speeds of up to a kilogram (just over 2 lb) a day. As adults they can reach more than 3 metres (10 ft) across and weigh an elephantine 2 tonnes, making them far and away the world's heaviest teleosts, or bony fish, as distinct from the soft-boned sharks and rays.

Sunfish evolved their unusual anatomy over time, as their ancestors lost their tails and gained a scalloped pseudotail, or clavus, that acts as a rudder. They propel themselves with their elongated dorsal and anal fins, which they swing from side to side with a sculling motion more like that of a sea turtle than a fish.

As well as *Mola mola*, there are at least three other species of sunfish. Most recently discovered is *M. tecta*, the hoodwinker sunfish, so named because for a long time it sneaked through the seas undetected. PhD researcher Marianne Nyegaard first caught a glimpse of the hidden species by studying DNA extracted from samples of sunfish skin. She found genetic sequences that didn't match any of the known species. Then, in 2014, after four years of searching for the mysterious sunfish, four of them washed up together on a beach in New Zealand.

Attenborough's Placoderm

Materpiscis attenboroughi

In the 1970s the broadcaster and biologist David Attenborough made a landmark BBC television series called *Life on Earth*. One episode featured an extraordinary collection of fish fossils from the Australian outback. A limestone escarpment, called the Gogo formation, marks where a huge barrier reef grew back in the Devonian period, some 380 million years ago. Swimming around it were ancient armoured fish, called placoderms, which have been exquisitely preserved inside rocky nodules. Palaeontologists crack these nodules open like Easter eggs to reveal the fossils inside.

Among the fossils is a fish inside a fish. At first it was thought to be the preserved remains of a predator's last meal, but on closer inspection it turned out to be an unborn embryo, still attached to its mother with an umbilical cord. The palaeontologist named it *Materpiscis* ('mother fish') *attenboroughi*, honouring the filmmaker's interest in the Gogo fossils. Attenborough later admitted that he was somewhat taken aback at having this particular fish named after him. This is the oldest known example of internal fertilization, and hence the first proof that ancient animals were getting together to have sex.

The palaeontologist who named *M. attenboroughi* also noticed L-shaped bones among other placoderm fossils and concluded that these were the equivalent of a male shark's claspers, used for transferring sperm to a female during copulation. He had uncovered fossilized remains of the world's oldest known genitalia.

These discoveries don't just tell us that there's been a long history of sex on Earth. They also reveal how adaptable animal mating strategies have been over the aeons. Most fish alive today belong to lineages that stopped copulating and went back to the more ancient approach of laying eggs.

Placoderms are no longer around, but they were the undisputed fishy rulers of Devonian seas. Some were tiny, some were flat like present-day stingrays, and some were truly enormous. *Dunkleosteus* was 6 metres (20 ft) long with a giant armoured head and ferocious jaws like massive, self-sharpening garden shears. At the time, sharks were only around a metre (3 ft) long and would have made an easy snack for a *Dunkleosteus*. It is thought that the only animals *Dunkleosteus* had to fear were each other. Fossils have been found with smashed armour plates punched with huge holes – the remnants of an epic battle between giants.

Chambered Nautilus

Nautilus pompilius

Both inside and out, the shell of a chambered nautilus is beautiful. Its ginger tiger stripes are a form of disguise, breaking up its outline and making it tricky for a predator to identify it from afar. Slicing an empty shell into two matching pieces, left and right, exposes an elegant spiral. This type of spiral (logarithmic) is common in nature, from spider webs to the spiralling arms of galaxies. It's based on a simple mathematical rule: the spiral must grow bigger by the same amount for every complete turn. A chambered nautilus does this by growing bigger itself and adding more calcium carbonate to its hard shell and inching its body forwards before sealing off a new chamber behind it.

There are six living species of nautilus. They are all varieties of cephalopod, together with their relatives the squid, octopuses, argonauts and cuttlefish. Nautiluses set themselves apart by being the only cephalopods that live permanently fixed inside a shell. They line their shells with shining nacre, or mother-of-pearl, which is where their other name comes from – the pearly nautilus. These gleaming, spiralling shells were very popular among Victorian collectors and were a common addition to cabinets of curiosities across Europe. Often nautilus 'cups' were etched with intricate designs and displayed in golden mounts.

In rocks around the world are masses of spiralling fossils that look a lot like nautiluses. In fact, these shells belonged to ancient relatives of theirs. Ammonites roamed Jurassic and Cretaceous seas in huge abundance and diversity, and their fossilized remains have revealed a lot about how the oceans used to be.

Ammonites ranged from coin-sized tiddlers to giants as big as monster-truck tyres. The biggest known fossil ammonite, *Parapuzosia seppenradensis*, was found in Germany and was probably at least 3 metres (nearly 10 ft) across when complete. Some ammonites didn't have smooth, spiralling shells but instead grew in strange shapes. *Helioceras* looked like spiny corkscrews, and they may have pirouetted up and down the water column. The shells of *Nipponites* were tightly knotted like a tangled vacuum-cleaner hose, while *Diplomoceras* looked like giant paperclips.

For millennia, people have found fossil ammonites and bestowed on them all manner of mysticism and meaning. Europeans commonly called them snakestones and often carved the missing head on to them. A seventh-century legend from the north of England tells how St Hilda established an abbey at Whitby and first rid the area of snakes by turning them to stone and hurling them off a cliff. Other stories tell of fairies being turned into snakes and then petrified. In parts of Scotland they were known as crampstones, and were placed in cows' drinking water in an attempt to cure the animals of cramp. People in ancient Rome believed they would see into the future if they slept with a golden ammonite (one covered in the shiny mineral pyrite) under their pillow. Black ammonites from the Himalayas are known as shaligrams and are sacred in Hindu culture as representations of the god Vishnu.

The name 'ammonite' stems from the Egyptian deity Amun, later adopted as Ammon by the ancient Greeks and commonly depicted with a pair of ram's horns. The Roman philosopher and naturalist Pliny the Elder was one of the first writers to make the connection between the ancient god's headgear and spiralling fossils.

A puzzle that palaeontologists ponder is why nautiluses are still alive today but nobody has ever seen a living ammonite. As far as we know, the last of the ammonites died 66 million years ago, around the same time as the dinosaurs. This was when a giant asteroid slammed into Earth and massive volcanoes erupted, emitting plumes of sulphur and carbon dioxide, which turned the seas acidic. One theory is that ammonite larvae were tiny and lived in shallow seas, and their shells may have corroded as the pH fell. Meanwhile, the ancestors of nautiluses may have survived thanks to their bigger, sturdier larvae and by living deep in the ocean, as chambered nautiluses do today.

The surviving nautilus lineage now faces more trouble. Their beautiful shells are still greatly desired as trinkets and decorations, and, rather than collecting empty shells that wash up on beaches, people now lower baited traps and catch live nautiluses from the deep. Consequently, after enduring several mass extinctions, chambered nautiluses must contend with another one, this time one caused by humans.

Giant Oarfish

Regalecus glesne

At up to 8 metres (just over 26 ft) from snout to tail tip, oarfish are the longest of all fish. They are also deeply mysterious, and are rarely seen alive. When these serpentine fish wash up on coastlines, often after storms, many people imagine they must have something important to tell us. In Japanese myths, a beached oarfish is a warning of impending disaster, most likely an earthquake. Researchers recently tested this idea, gathering reported strandings of oarfish and other fish from deep waters and comparing them to the occurrence of major earthquakes. Out of hundreds of reports going back to the 1920s, only a single case located an oarfish stranding within 30 days and 100 kilometres (62 miles) of an earthquake epicentre. Otherwise, there's no hint that seismic stirrings disturb deep-dwelling fish so much that they dash to the surface and hurl themselves on to dry land.

Oarfish get their name from times before anyone had seen one alive, when people thought they swam by rowing through the water with their pelvic fins, which trail like streamers. Contemporary footage from deep-diving submersibles has revealed that in fact oarfish hold their bodies poker-straight and rhythmically undulate the dorsal fin that runs all the way along their back. To feed, they hang vertically with their heads up, perhaps so that they can make out the silhouettes of squid, fish and shrimp in the water above them. Having such a long body evidently has its drawbacks. Most stranded oarfish show signs that at some point they've self-amputated part of their tails. Maybe, like lizards and geckos, they do that to distract an attacker and make a getaway. But unlike those reptiles, oarfish can't grow their tails back.

Sea Cucumbers

Holothuroidea

There's much more to sea cucumbers than immediately meets the eye. Admittedly, many are not especially endearing. They lie on the sandy seabed like giant, lazy worms, and when they're disturbed, they shoot their intestines out of their backsides, releasing a tangle of sticky threads. Some, however, are quite handsome and look like enlarged versions of colourful sea slugs. Those known as sea apples (*Pseudocolochirus axiologus*) are purple and red with hundreds of yellow tubular feet and a crown of bushy yellow tentacles. Leopard sea cucumbers (*Bohadschia argus*) have fine orange spots, and in the deep sea lives a translucent yellow species (*Psychropotes longicauda*) with a long 'tail', nicknamed the gummy squirrel. Swimming sea cucumbers (*Pelagothuria natatrix*) look more like diaphanous jellyfish. And you can take a guess as to why another deep-sea swimmer (*Enypniastes eximia*) was nicknamed the headless chicken monster.

Sea cucumbers belong to the same group as starfish and sea urchins, and there are more than 1,000 species around the world. For centuries they've made an impression on human lives via the trade in the Asian delicacy known as *trepang* or *bêche-de-mer*. Salted and dried, sea cucumbers are prized as a culinary ingredient and aphrodisiac. A dish known as 'Buddha Jumps Over the Wall' blends animal ingredients including shark fin and sea cucumber, and is apparently so delicious it would tempt vegetarian Buddhist monks to climb the walls of their temples to get some.

In the eighteenth century sea-cucumber fishing was focused on the island of Sulawesi in Indonesia, and expanded into northern Australia. Today, with strong demand from the Chinese middle classes, it has gone global. Fishers as far away as Spain have begun targeting them, prices have rocketed, and some species sell for thousands of dollars per kilogram. Organized crime gangs have got involved, and now poaching and smuggling are rife. In many places, sea cucumber populations are disappearing, and they're very much missed by the ecosystems they leave behind.

Similar to the way earthworms support healthy soils, sea cucumbers help to keep ocean ecosystems healthy. Many species are excellent bioturbators, that is to say, they bury themselves in sand and mud, aerating and mixing the sediment. Scientists estimate that the reef surrounding Heron Island on the Great Barrier Reef is home to 3 million sea cucumbers that collectively pass 64,000 tonnes of sediment through their guts every year. Sea cucumbers clean up sediment and recycle nutrients. They release calcium carbonate, which helps corals grow. More than 200 species of animal live on and inside sea cucumbers, including snails, crabs, shrimp, worms and even other sea cucumbers. Pearlfish (Carapidae) live on the respiratory tree, the sea cucumbers' breathing organs, which are located just inside their anus. To get in and out, pearlfish simply wait for the sea cucumber to take a breath.

Clown Anemonefish

Amphiprion ocellaris

Thanks to a certain animated Pixar movie, several species of coral-reef fish have become famous – especially the one with distinctive orange-and-white stripes, the clown anemonefish (also known as the clownfish). The story of the anemonefish called Nemo who gets lost contains a good number of accurate biological facts. Female anemonefish do indeed lay clutches of eggs near an anemone, and they are at grave risk of predation (Nemo lost all his siblings). However, the filmmakers steered away from some of the details that would have made for a rather different story. For instance, when Nemo's mother disappeared, his father would have spontaneously undergone a sex change, turned into a female and taken over as boss of the anemone.

A strict hierarchy exists among anemonefish. Each anemone is home to a single female. She is always the largest, dominant fish and her mate is a large male. The rest of the anemonefish are subordinates that don't yet mate, as either males or females. You can work out where each of them lies in the pecking order by their size: the smallest are the newcomers at the bottom of the hierarchy, followed by slightly bigger and bigger ones. Line them up and they look like Russian dolls in fish form, with the smaller ones identical miniature versions of the higher-ranking fish.

The threat of being kicked out of the anemone by the more dominant fish is enough to keep the subordinates in line. They adjust how much they eat to stay small, waiting their turn to climb the social ladder. It can take 10 or even 20 years for an anemonefish to rise to the top and become one of the two biggest fish – the ones that get to breed. The reason they wait is because there is a limited supply of anemone real estate to move into. Anemonefish do best to find an anemone with a queue that isn't too long, and hang around for as long as it takes.

Besides persuading cinemagoers to fall in love with these adorable orange fish, *Finding Nemo* also showcases an iconic example of symbiosis. The fact that anemonefish have adopted these particular host animals to live with is remarkable. Normally anemones kill and eat small fish. Anemones are close relatives of corals and jellyfish, and like them they have stinging nematocyst cells that paralyse prey. It's still something of a mystery how exactly anemonefish make themselves immune to the stingers, but it's likely that slime plays a part. The fish can be seen vigorously rubbing themselves around the base of their anemone, spreading slime over their skin. One idea is that the slime layer becomes so thick that it blocks the stings. Another is that somehow chemicals in the slime trick the anemone into thinking the fish are just wriggling parts of their own body, so they don't attack.

What is clear is that this is a true partnership from which both fish and anemones gain. For the fish, the stinging tentacles give them a safe home — so much so that they've become completely dependent on their anemones and can't survive without one. The anemones also survive better and grow bigger when they have fish living with them. During the day, anemonefish chase off butterflyfish that like to nibble on anemone tentacles. At night, the fish hunker down among the tentacles, where they don't fall sound asleep but keep wriggling. This brings in fresh, oxygen-rich seawater, which helps the anemones breathe and grow. Anemonefish pee is also good for anemones, since it contains nitrogen that fertilizes tiny algae living inside the tentacles. This is another symbiotic partnership: the algae live safely inside the anemone, producing oxygen and sugars that help the anemone to grow.

Pom Pom Crab

Lybia tessellata

A study in 1880 of crustaceans living around Mauritius and the Seychelles in the Indian Ocean made brief reference to a small crab that grabs a living sea anemone in each claw and waves them around. This was the first report of the unusual behaviour of pom pom crabs, also known as boxer crabs (search online and you'll find gifs that show their splendid side-to-side cheerleading). The crabs have come to depend entirely on their living boxing gloves, and have never been spotted in the wild without a pair. They carefully hold on to the anemones with specialized hooks, which make their claws no use for anything else.

In laboratories, when scientists take away one of a crab's anemones, it will simply rip the other one in two. The split anemone pieces then regenerate into two whole animals. Likewise, anemone-free crabs will fight other crabs and steal one or both of their anemones. Crabs wave their stinging gloves at each other during a stand-off before a fight, but they rarely come to blows or use them as weapons. They use anemones chiefly to get food and sting their prey before eating it.

The anemones gain some benefits from being grabbed by a crab. They get to travel and breathe better in more oxygen-rich water, which can otherwise stagnate around them (it's the same reason that anemones grow better with fidgeting clownfish). But their food supply is severely curtailed. When scientists took anemones away from their crabs, they almost tripled in size. It turns out the crabs steal the anemones' food – right out of their mouths – to keep them small enough to hold on to. These are bonsai anemones.

Other crabs, generally known as decorator crabs, gather up various animals and algae, fixing them to their shells with bristles that act like Velcro. These decorations can be for camouflage or defence. Some crabs cover their whole bodies in sea anemones, some walk around with spiky sea urchins on their backs, some pick brightly coloured, noxious sponges that warn predators to stay away, and some drape themselves in so much seaweed it's hard to tell there's a crab underneath at all.

Mudskipper

Oxudercidae

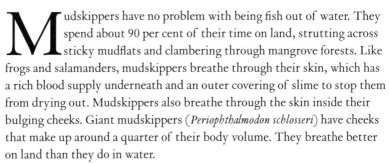

Mudskippers have no problem with being fish out of water. They spend about 90 per cent of their time on land, strutting across sticky mudflats and clambering through mangrove forests. Like frogs and salamanders, mudskippers breathe through their skin, which has a rich blood supply underneath and an outer covering of slime to stop them from drying out. Mudskippers also breathe through the skin inside their bulging cheeks. Giant mudskippers (*Periophthalmodon schlosseri*) have cheeks that make up around a quarter of their body volume. They breathe better on land than they do in water.

Also like amphibians, mudskippers have froggy eyes perched high on their heads, which let them peep out of water. Each eye swivels, giving them almost 360-degree vision. Mudskippers prevent their eyes from drying out by dipping them down into liquid-filled cups on their heads.

More than 30 species of mudskipper live around the world between the tides, all of them types of goby. Many are highly territorial and aggressively chase off intruders. During the mating season, male mudskippers develop bright-blue spots on their skin and perform impressive jumping contests, presumably to impress females by trying to leap the highest. Boddart's goggle-eyed gobies (*Boleophthalmus boddarti*) build little walls of mud to cordon off their territory. Like garden fences, these help the fish to live peacefully alongside their neighbours. When scientists removed these walls, the mudskippers became much angrier with each other, until they rebuilt their partitions and calmed down again.

Mudskippers are among at least 12 groups of living fish that have taken steps towards land. None of them is the fish that originally crawled out of the sea and gave rise to all land-dwelling vertebrates: the amphibians, reptiles, birds and mammals. That happened around 400 million years ago, when distant ancestors of living fish (called tetrapods) made a permanent break for land. Mudskippers and other amphibious fish evolved much more recently to live partially out of water, but they offer clues about how those ancient animals probably went about making this transition. Scientists recently sequenced the DNA of several mudskipper species and found changes in their genes, including those helping them to see out of water and those boosting their immunity against diseases they might catch as they move on to land.

Landlubbing fish must also learn to walk. Mudskippers use their pectoral fins like stiff crutches and propel themselves with their powerful tails. Freshwater fish from rivers and swamps in Africa, called bichirs (in the family Polypteridae), look like little smiling snakes covered in shining scales. If water levels recede, they scramble along on their pectoral fins and quickly get better at walking. When scientists have kept bichirs in humid aquarium tanks with no access to water, within a year they adopt a more efficient gait. The fish walk with their heads held high, they plant their fins more firmly on the ground, and their muscles and bones adapt to a walking lifestyle.

Probably the most agile walking fish are those that can climb up waterfalls. Nopoli rock-climbing gobies (*Sicyopterus stimpsoni*) are endemic to Hawaii, where they're known as *'o'opu nōpili*. They climb against the flow of water, inching their way up using their mouths and suckers made from pelvic fins. These finger-sized fish can climb waterfalls hundreds of metres high. They do it to lay their eggs upstream. When they hatch, the young fish are immediately swept down the waterfall and out into the ocean. Six months later, when they're bigger, they climb all the way back up again.

As well as fish that breathe air like frogs, various species have lungs that may have evolved first, then adapted later into the gas-filled flotation device a lot of fish still have, the swim bladder. Many fish with lungs are obligate air-breathers, including lungfish (in the subclass Dipnoi) and bichirs, and suffocate if they can't get to the surface. These are fish that can drown.

Money Cowrie

Monetaria moneta

There's something pleasing about the feel and sound of a handful of small cowrie shells, like smooth marbles clinking together. In life, money cowries cover their shells in a soft mantle with delicate zebra stripes, which helps to keep them smooth and shiny. They live on tropical coral reefs, tucked away in crevices, and their empty shells commonly wash up on beaches.

People around the world, even far from the ocean, have used cowries as decorations, as symbols of purity, fertility and renewal. Cowries have been placed over the eyes of dead people in their graves. An ancient group of horse-riding nomads of central Asia, the Scythians, may never have seen the ocean, but buried their dead with cowries. And for centuries people on the Indian Ocean islands of the Maldives gathered cowries by throwing coconut palms into the sea, among which the little snails would creep and hide. Maldivian cowries were sent to India, to trade for rice and cloth. Arab traders also took cowries from India to Egypt and as far as West Africa, where, in the fourteenth century, cowries were adopted as currency.

The cowrie trade remained relatively modest until European traders came on to the scene and found their own, grim use for the shells. Dutch and British merchants sailed to South East Asia and China to buy tea, spices and silk, then called in at Indian ports to load up on cheap cowrie shells, which were used as ballast to keep their ships steady in the heaving waves. The cowries were unloaded in Europe then repacked to take to West Africa, where they were used to buy humans.

During the transatlantic slave trade, the price per person went up from around 10,000 to 160,000 cowries. In total, some 30 billion Maldivian cowries were traded in West Africa for people. When the slave trade finally ended, cowries were instead exchanged for palm oil grown in West African plantations. A second cowrie species, gold ringers (*Monetaria annulus*) from Zanzibar, entered the trade in the nineteenth century. Within 20 years some 16 billion gold ringers had flooded the market, causing hyperinflation and devaluation, until cowries were once again nothing more than a pleasing handful of smooth shapes.

Giant Moray Eel

Gymnothorax javanicus

Moray eels are formidable nocturnal predators on coral reefs, with a few characteristics that make them especially dangerous for other fish. Not only do their mouths bristle with sharp fangs, but also they have a second set of teeth lodged further back, called pharyngeal jaws. These are similar to the jaws that parrotfish use to grind up corals and crunchy seaweeds. Moray eels' jaws are raptorial. They evolved to shoot forwards and seize prey then pull it down their throat, a unique behaviour among animals. *Alien* monster, eat your heart out.

What's more, the moray eels' long, slender bodies allow them to slip into the crevices of reefs and chase prey that might otherwise think it can hide in safety. This is why another coral-reef predator, the roving grouper (*Plectropomus pessuliferus*), learned to hunt with giant moray eels. Such interspecies collaboration is rare, especially among fish. Groupers actively seek out moray eels in their daytime resting places. They swim right up to a moray eel and shake their head rapidly from side to side. It's quite unusual in the animal kingdom for different species to communicate like this. Seeing the grouper's signal, the moray eel stirs itself and they swim off together to go hunting. The fast-swimming grouper chases after prey fish. If the prey slips into the reef, the moray eel dives after it and either eats it or flushes it out for the waiting grouper to gobble. The grouper also has better eyesight than the eel. If it knows where a fish is hiding it will point it out to the eel, gesturing with its snout. Scientists have observed the grouper–eel hunting team for hours and noted that both species do better and get more to eat in this way than when they hunt alone.

Around the world there are at least 200 species of moray eel, some in temperate seas but most on tropical coral reefs, where they can be seen having their teeth cleaned by cleaner wrasse. Various species, especially the snowflake moray (*Echidna nebulosa*), with its bright-yellow eyes and mottled skin, are popular among aquarium keepers.

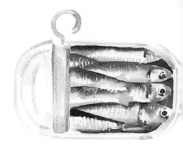

INDIAN OCEAN (AND WORLDWIDE)

Southern African Pilchard

Sardinops sagax

Roughly a quarter of all the fish species that swim through the seas do so in close company of other fish. When left on their own they immediately grow agitated. Some of the most impressive are pilchards and sardines – interchangeable names for a variety of small, silvery fish species that live permanently together in shoals and schools. Each year from May to July a spectacular sardine run sweeps along the southeastern coast of Africa. Billions of Southern African pilchards congregate to spawn and migrate northwards in cool waters that stream from the Agulhas Bank towards Mozambique. Such a rich bounty of fish is a major attraction for all sorts of predators. Bryde's whales, cape gannets, common dolphins and bronze whaler sharks all join the melee.

The difference between a shoal and a school is simply a matter of organization. In a shoal, the fish are all hanging out together and generally heading in the same direction; a shoal transforms into a school when the fish coordinate their movements more closely, often swimming towards or away from somewhere specific.

As pilchards and other fish swim in tightly coordinated schools, they seem to become part of a single-minded super-organism that thinks as one. But in fact, each fish makes its own decisions about the speed and direction to swim in. One of the simple rules is always to stay two body lengths away from the fish in front. Pressure-sensitive pores along the fish's bodies allow them to detect the positions of those around them. Individual fish also have their preferred place within a school: some like to lead and others are content to follow. They also tend to hang out on either the left- or the right-hand side of the school.

Swimming in shoals and schools comes with various benefits, the most obvious being the general rule of safety in numbers. By blending in with a crowd of similar-sized and -shaped fish, an individual is much less likely to be singled out and caught. Swimming together also saves energy, like cycling in a peloton. Scientists studying the formation of fish schools have found that individuals place themselves in precisely the right spot to gain an extra push from the turbulent wake created by their neighbours. Mimicking this in wind farms, by placing turbines in a similar arrangement, leads to more efficient generation of energy.

When schooling fish come under attack they become even better coordinated, splitting in two as a shark or dolphin races through, then re-forming behind them. And when danger heightens, the school closes in on itself into a swirling, frenzied bait ball. Each fish dives into the centre of the sphere, trying to hide behind its schoolmates and get as far as possible from the hunters' jaws. Often, however, the whole bait ball succumbs, as a pod of dolphins picks them all off from below and the sides, and diving birds plunge from above, or a huge baleen whale comes along and swallows the entire school in one gulp.

Humans have also benefited from the shoaling and schooling behaviour of fish. It's what allows fishing nets to scoop up huge numbers of fish in one go. Especially important throughout the history of fishing are forage fish, a term for pilchards, sardines, sprat, herring, anchovies, shad, menhaden and others that are preyed on by larger marine predators. Forage fish were made into ancient Roman fermented fish sauce, were a medieval staple food and have been packed tight into endless cans, and are now the target of industrial super-trawlers used in the largest fisheries in the world. Of the total global catch of wild fish, at least a third is forage fish. Around 90 per cent of them are turned into fish meal and fish oil to feed to livestock, including pigs, poultry and salmon in fish farms. Many people think we'd be better off eating the forage fish ourselves.

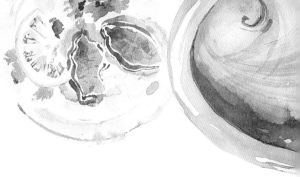

Abalone

Haliotis spp.

Abalone are flattened sea snails, shaped like ears, that people have known about and used for a long time. In Blombos Cave, South Africa, archaeologists found two South African abalone shells (*Haliotis midae*) which were used 100,000 years ago as paint pots. They were part of a paint-making toolkit that somebody used to grind ochre with charcoal and seal bones, possibly heating the mixture and using the abalone shells with their holes plugged to store the red pigment. The finding provided more evidence that even at this early stage in the evolution of *Homo sapiens*, people planned and produced things, and figured out that palm-sized abalone shells can be useful containers.

A major use of abalone today is for their lustrous, oily nacre, often in deep greens and blues, to make jewellery and inlays. In Aotearoa (New Zealand), abalone are known as *pāua* and recognized as *taonga*, treasures in Maori culture.

People also have a long history of eating abalone, because these meaty snails are easy to find along the shoreline and prise from rocks. Abalone remains a delicacy, and in some places it has declined from overzealous collecting. In 2001 white abalone (*H. sorenseni*) was the first marine invertebrate to be added to the United States' Endangered Species List, after decades of over-fishing almost wiped it out. In California's Channel Islands there used to be about 12,500 of them per hectare (5,000 per acre) of seabed, but now you'll be lucky to find a single one in the same area. Despite protection, the species is still struggling because the remaining abalone are too widely dispersed to breed with each other. Efforts are now underway to breed them in captivity and release them back into the wild.

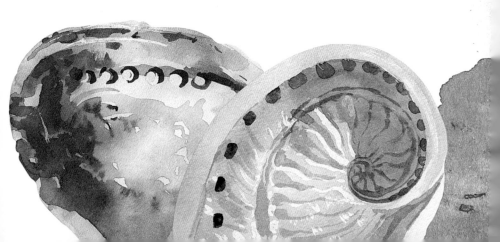

Parrotfish

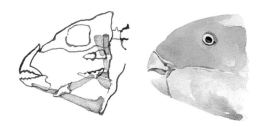

Scaridae

White sandy beaches and coral atolls are the epitome of tropical paradise, and they wouldn't exist without fish. Parrotfish are responsible for generating a large portion of the gleaming sand that dusts the feet of strolling holidaymakers. On Vakkru Island in the Maldives, scientists analysed the sand's origins in detail and discovered that parrotfish make up around 85 per cent of the sand. Visitors may be shocked, but really they should be grateful to these fish for the role they play in turning coral into pulverized, powdery sand. The truth of the matter is that white tropical sands are mostly made up of parrotfish poo.

About 100 species of parrotfish live on coral reefs, seagrass meadows and rocky coasts around the world. They're easily distinguished by their characteristic teeth, which are fused into a parrot-like beak. Each fish has 1,000 teeth that are lined up in 15 rows and cemented together to form a super-tough structure. Worn teeth drop out and are replaced by the next ones in line, in a similar way to sharks' teeth.

Most parrotfish are herbivores and feed on fleshy seaweeds that grow on reefs. As they graze and munch, they can't help but scrape up limestone from the old, dead coral skeletons underneath. Scuba divers who have visited coral reefs will be familiar with the grating sound of feeding parrotfish. Some species, including the biggest, the bumphead parrotfish, feed on live corals and crunch mouthfuls to extract the thin layer of living tissue on the corals' microscopic polyps.

At the back of their throats, parrotfish have a second set of teeth, as if they were trying to swallow a pair of dentures. Known as the pharyngeal jaws, these grind up coral into a fine powder before the fish swallows. Then the coral-seaweed mix passes through the parrotfish's guts, where nutrients are digested and eventually the powdery limestone remains emerge from the other end as a trickle of fine sand.

With their endless munching and defecating, parrotfish are ecological engineers. On Palmyra Atoll in the Pacific Ocean, snorkelling scientists followed bumphead parrotfish as they went about their days, and counted up their bodily functions. On average, these metre-long (3 ft) fish take three bites of coral every minute and poo 20 times an hour. Over the course of a year, a single bumphead eats between 4 and 6 tonnes of coral. That is a lot of sand.

Like their feathered namesakes, parrotfish come dressed in various flamboyant colours. Most change their appearance and their sex during their lifetime, often starting as monochromatic females, then flourishing as rainbow-coloured males. Some will even change sex again and go back to being female. Brightest are the so-called super males that lead harems of females. When night falls, parrotfish find themselves quiet places on the seabed to settle down. They secrete a mucus bubble around themselves, which protects them from nocturnal bloodsucking snails. Safely tucked up inside their gooey sleeping bags, parrotfish fall sound asleep.

As well as making sand and building beaches and islands, parrotfish are tremendously important for the health of coral reefs. These grazing herbivores ensure corals don't become overgrown by algae. And the scraping fish leave clean surfaces on the solid base of old coral below, where coral larvae can drift in, settle and grow into new colonies. In Panama, the fossilized remains of reefs have shown that for millennia corals and parrotfish have been locked together in an ebbing and flowing dance. Whenever parrotfish populations were abundant and healthy, so were corals; when parrotfish numbers fell – including during the last 200 years of over-fishing – corals grew more slowly and lost their vibrant health. One of the most effective ways of protecting coral reefs is to protect parrotfish from being fished and to make sure there are plenty swimming about in big shoals.

Barreleye

Macropinna microstoma

In the inky depths of the twilight zone, between 600 and 800 metres (1,970–2,625 ft) down, there are fish with remarkable emerald eyes. Barreleyes have been known of since 1939, when specimens were caught in nets and brought to the surface. The two small spots above a barreleye's mouth that look like eyes are in fact olfactory organs, called nares, that sniff chemicals in the water. In the fish's real eyes, the green pigments may filter out the dim sunlight that trickles into the twilight zone, giving them a better chance of glimpsing the flashing bioluminescent lights of other animals.

Scientists who first pondered these odd-looking fish assumed that their domed green eyes were fixed, permanently gazing up to spot the silhouettes of prey above them. The tubular shape of the fish's eyes allows them to detect very low light levels, but it restricts their field of view. Then, in 2009, a living barreleye was caught on camera by a deep-diving robot off the Californian coast, and scientists realized two things. Firstly, the fish's peculiar eyes can actually swivel. When a barreleye spots something of interest it rotates its eyes like a pair of binoculars. Second, the scientists saw a large transparent dome over their heads, like a cartoon space helmet or an upturned goldfish bowl. The delicate structure had been torn off the collected specimens. Seeing this intact gave scientists a clue as to what barreleyes eat. Nobody has yet seen this happening, but it's possible they swim up to the great long bodies of deep-sea siphonophores and steal small prey snagged in their tentacles. The clear dome protects the fish's green eyes from the stings.

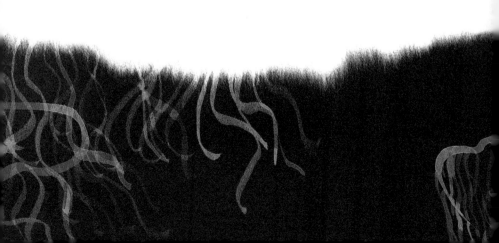

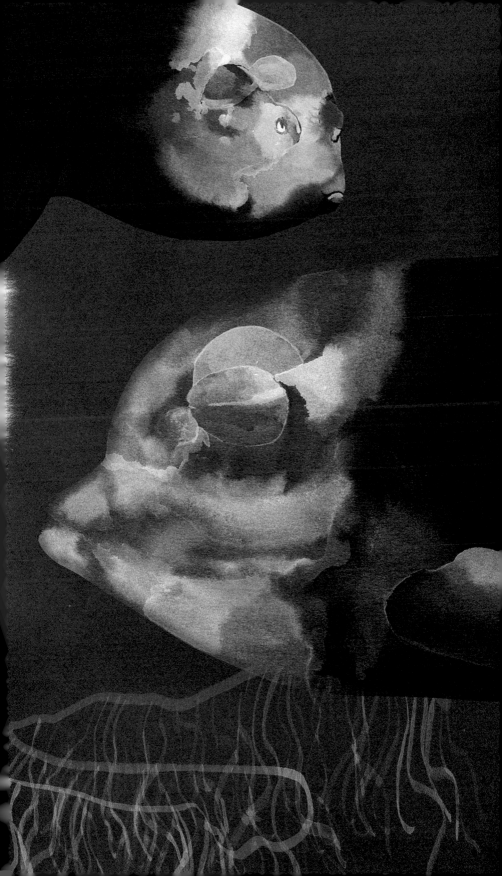

Walking Shark

Hemiscyllium spp.

Several big myths surrounding sharks are well and truly busted by one particular group of these toothy predators. For starters, walking sharks show that not all sharks have to keep swimming in order to breathe. They lie on their bellies and snooze through the day, pumping water over their gills. Then, at nightfall, they stir themselves into action and, as their name suggests, they have the unusual habit of walking across the seabed, wriggling like a salamander and using their paddle-shaped fins as rudimentary legs. They can even hold their breath for at least an hour at a time. All this means they can clamber between tide pools that get cut off as the sea retreats, and feast on the stranded fish, crustaceans and worms that have no way to escape.

Biologists recently discovered that there are not five, as previously thought, but nine species of walking sharks living in northern Australia, Papua New Guinea and Indonesia. Distinct skin patterns help us to tell the different walking sharks apart, with combinations of leopard spots, zebra stripes and black dots like squirts from a spray can. The best known are the epaulette sharks, which have two large spots that look a bit like military shoulder decorations.

Messages written into the walking sharks' DNA have revealed an unexpected truth: these are the ocean's newest sharks. The genus is nine million years old. The youngest two species split apart less than two million years ago, when *Homo habilis*, our not-too-distant human ancestors, were busy splitting pebbles into sharp tools. This date challenges the lingering idea that all sharks are ancient and unchanging.

Sharks have been around for 450 million years and some species have seemingly remained immutable for great portions of time, sticking to the winning model of streamlined predator. But walking sharks do things differently. They don't move far or fast. Adults perform bizarre mating rituals standing on their heads. The resulting fertilized eggs hatch into mini-adults that immediately begin their pedestrian lives. As if proving the point of their sedentary nature, one species of walking shark got where it is today in central Indonesia by hitching a ride on its home island, which migrated westwards on a sliding tectonic plate.

Banded Archerfish

Toxotes jaculatrix

There's a long-held belief that because fish have small, relatively simple brains they aren't as smart as other vertebrates, especially mammals. This assumption subtly influences the way people feel about fish and how we treat them. But various fish demonstrate impressive mental prowess, and none quite as flamboyantly as the archerfish.

In tropical mangroves, the archerfish prowls around peering through the waterline, searching for insects perched on surrounding vegetation. When it finds a target, this little fish performs a series of mental calculations. It considers the way light bends as it passes from air into water, gauges the distance and angle to shoot, and predicts where to wait for its falling prey. Then the archerfish raises its lips to the surface and fires a water bullet, shooting a doomed insect from up to 3 metres (10 ft) away, impressive for a 20-centimetre (8 in) fish. The instant it shoots, the archerfish shimmies its fins in a fine-tuned movement to overcome the recoil. Then, within milliseconds, the archerfish darts forwards and swallows its prey.

Archerfish also manipulate water to make it useful. An archerfish pushes water along a groove in the roof of its mouth using its tongue. Critically, it pushes harder towards the end of a water jet so that droplets further back go faster and the stream merges into a single, speeding bullet. This trick lets archerfish shoot water with more than five times the power they could muster if they were simply using their muscles.

These fishy assassins also show another aspect to their mental abilities. Scientists at Oxford University trained them with food to shoot at particular human faces on a computer screen. Later, when shown a mixture of faces, the fish still knew which one to hit in order to be rewarded with a snack. They could even do it when the faces were turned at different angles. Fish lack a neocortex, the part of the brain that humans use for recognizing faces. Human facial recognition is not important for fish, but still they can perform these complicated visual tasks. It's clear that there's a lot more going on inside a fish's mind than we might at first imagine.

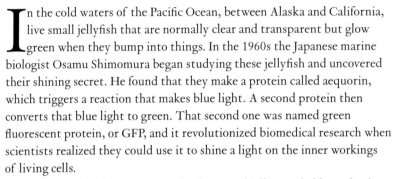

Crystal Jelly

Aequorea victoria

In the cold waters of the Pacific Ocean, between Alaska and California, live small jellyfish that are normally clear and transparent but glow green when they bump into things. In the 1960s the Japanese marine biologist Osamu Shimomura began studying these jellyfish and uncovered their shining secret. He found that they make a protein called aequorin, which triggers a reaction that makes blue light. A second protein then converts that blue light to green. That second one was named green fluorescent protein, or GFP, and it revolutionized biomedical research when scientists realized they could use it to shine a light on the inner workings of living cells.

Like many bioluminescent animals, crystal jellies probably evolved their glowing proteins as a form of defence, to startle predators. For scientists, the useful thing GFP does is to glow when blue or ultraviolet light shines on it. The gene for GFP can be inserted into cells or whole living bodies, and wherever it goes, it glows. Crucially, researchers can attach GFP to other genes and proteins, then easily track them through a cell or body just by shining light on them. GFP essentially works as a glow-in-the-dark tag, and it's proved to be a powerful research tool, being used to track the spread of cancer cells and to study other diseases as well as stem cells and developing embryos.

There's now a whole rainbow palette of fluorescent proteins that scientists have extracted from various sea creatures, including corals, sea anemones and plankton. These have been used to create a menagerie of genetically engineered glow-in-the-dark animals – ones that don't naturally glow. Among the first were zebrafish, which were developed as detectors for environmental pollution. They were injected with GFP so that they glowed when they swam through contaminated water. In 2011 a team of scientists inserted a gene into cats that helped them to resist the feline version of HIV/AIDS, and tagged it with GFP to see how it spread through their bodies. There have also been glowing sheep, rabbits, marmosets, dogs and pigs, and, of course, neon mice. Many of these have genuine scientific applications, but you can also now buy yourself a glowing pet fish.

Mandarinfish

Synchiropus splendidus

At sundown on coral reefs from Japan to Australia, male mandarinfish emerge from their hiding places and flaunt their exuberant colours and patterns, fluttering their fins to attract the attention of females. Dazzling oranges and greens across their bodies and fins are offset by squiggles of intense ultramarine. For female mandarinfish it's an irresistible combination. Each picks a colourful mate and perches on his outstretched pectoral fin. Then the pair rise up together to release eggs and sperm that mingle in the water.

Bright colours play an important role in the mating rituals of mandarinfish, but they also catch the eye of intruders, including those that gladly snack on little fish. That being so, mandarinfish have evolved a counterstrategy. They may look gorgeous, but they smell terrible, being covered in an evil-smelling, toxic mucus that acts as an effective predator repellent. Indeed, the mandarinfish's eye-catching coloration could serve a dual purpose: to attract mates and warn predators to stay away.

Among the mandarinfish's patterns, the most remarkable is the intense blue. It just so happens that being truly blue is rare among animals. Mandarinfish are one of very few species – and only two fish – that produce blue pigments, the other fish being the picturesque dragonet, a close relative of the mandarinfish. Most other blue animal body parts, from butterfly wings to human eyes, are more of an illusion of blue, being made of structured materials that scatter and interfere with light in such a way as to appear blue. Crush the scales of a butterfly's wings and it will lose its structure and with it its colour. Not so for the mandarinfish, which have real blue pigments in their skin, like paint.

Humphead Wrasse

Cheilinus undulatus

Gaze at a fully grown male humphead wrasse and you may get a sense of an animal that's watching you just as closely as you are watching him. Maybe it's because there's something of the doleful puppy in his demeanour, with those big eyes and that forward-sloping snout. Or maybe it's simply because he is so very big. With large size comes a certain dignified grandeur. He's longer than your outstretched arms, and he'd have trouble fitting in a bathtub. Except for sharks, no other fish on coral reefs grow bigger. Across his face is a tangled maze of blue-green patterns that are his alone. Each humphead wrasse comes with unique decorations, like a fingerprint on their face. A faceprint.

This means that if you wanted to, you could track an individual humphead wrasse through its long, complicated life. To begin with is the juvenile phase, speckled in black and white, then after a few years the fish changes into a sage-green female. Several decades later she may undertake one more dramatic transformation. A blue bump swells on her head and she changes sex.

For wrasse and various other fish families, it's quite normal to experience both sexes and swap between the two, either male then female, or female then male, or both at once. Sex-changing behaviour evolved because it gives the fish an advantage of some sort. For humphead wrasse, it's probably to do with the unusual way they spawn. Usually they're solitary, but when the moon is full they gather in shoals in a particular spot on the reef that's guarded by a dominant male wrasse. He patrols his territory, rounding up a harem of dozens of females. When they decide the time is right, the females take turns to join him for a few brief moments and each presses her delicate body close to his, several times her size. She releases a cloud of eggs into the sea, he releases sperm, and immediately the pair separate, leaving the drifting embryos to start life by themselves. The female goes about her day on the reef and the male turns his attention to the next female. He'll keep going until there's no one left to mate with.

Being able to change sex means that a population should have the right balance of females and males. Only one dominant male is needed to mate with lots of females; a few subordinate males hang around, sneaking in now and then to mate with females, but basically they're waiting to move up the hierarchy and eventually take charge.

These spawning spectacles are now rare and happen only in well-protected parts of the ocean. Throughout their range in the Indo-Pacific, especially in Indonesia, Malaysia and the Philippines, humphead wrasse have been hunted for a global trade in live fish. A common way to catch them involves divers using hookah equipment, breathing from a hosepipe connected to an air compressor on a boat. They chase wrasse into crevices in a reef, then squirt a solution of cyanide to knock them out but not kill them. The fish are then kept in a flooded compartment on the boat. Some are destined for public aquaria, but most end up in Asian restaurants, where diners pay top dollar to pick out the fish they want killed and cooked. Humphead wrasse are highly prized. A special delicacy is a plate of the males' big, rubbery lips.

The international trade now far outpaces traditional fisheries in a few Pacific islands where humphead wrasse are highly respected. In Papua New Guinea, only village elders are allowed to eat them. In Guam, it was once a rite of passage for young men to spear a humphead wrasse underwater, and in the Cook Islands, they were traditionally caught for royal feasts. Their cultural significance among Fijians is commemorated on one of the country's coins.

Once it became clear how fast global trade was wiping out the highly endangered humphead wrasse, some countries restricted exports or banned them altogether. But demand remains high and wrasse are traded on the black market. Conservationists have now developed a smartphone app to track the illegal trade. Members of the public take photographs of wrasse in restaurant aquariums and an algorithm identifies individuals based on their intricate facial patterns. Information collected by the app has revealed that restaurant owners with a licence for a single wrasse regularly sell them and swap in other, illegal fish.

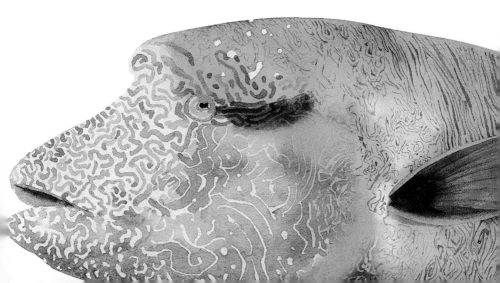

Totoaba and Vaquita

Totoaba macdonaldi and *Phocoena sinus*

In the Gulf of California, in Mexico, lives a large fish species that's being driven to extinction because one of its internal organs is worth more than its weight in gold. Totoaba swim bladders can sell for as much as $80,000 a kilo (gold generally hovers around the $50,000–60,000 mark). These gas-filled balloons are a common feature in fish and serve various purposes, including buoyancy control and acting as a sound-generating and -detecting device. In China, dried fish swim bladders, also known as maws, are a delicacy and are made into soup with supposed medicinal powers. Totoabas have been over-fished for decades, and since 1975 it's been illegal to catch them, but high demand continues to drive a rampant black market. Illegal consignments of swim bladders, often stuffed into suitcases, are regularly confiscated, including from totoaba trafficking syndicates that smuggle the valuable fish parts out of Mexico. It's not known how many totoaba are left.

Illegal fishing is causing the precipitous demise not only of the 2-metre-long (6½ ft) totoabas, but also of the world's smallest and rarest porpoise – the vaquita. With dark patches around their eyes, vaquita have been nicknamed the pandas of the sea, but they are far more endangered than the bamboo-eating mammals.

Like totoaba, vaquita are endemic to the Gulf of California, and they too easily get caught and drowned in the gillnets illegally set to catch migrating totoaba between November and May each year. In 1997 scientists estimated that there were 567 vaquitas in the wild. In 2018 the population count had dropped to 19. By 2021 there were thought to be only 9 left. Efforts to breed vaquita in captivity have been a dismal failure. There is, however, a glimmer of hope that the species is not doomed to extinction. There could be several young vaquita in the population, and scientists think females may be able to produce a calf every year, rather than every two years as previously thought. A recent study also suggests that the remaining vaquita have enough genetic diversity to keep the population going. The key to saving vaquita will be to stop killing them and to end the illegal totoaba trade.

Yeti Crab

Kiwa hirsuta

On a hydrothermal vent field in the Pacific Ocean, some way south of Easter Island, live a particular type of striking white crab. Deep-sea scientists named them *Kiwa hirsuta*: *Kiwa* after a Polynesian sea deity, and *hirsuta* meaning 'hairy' in Latin, owing to the luxuriant fur that sprouts on their arms (it's not actually fur, but extensions of their carapace). The crabs came to be commonly known as yeti crabs – just look at those long, hairy arms and you'll see why.

These crabs' furry appendages are key to their survival on hydrothermal vents. Like the scaly-foot snails, yeti crabs rely on chemical-harnessing bacteria for food. But rather than having the bacteria grow inside their bodies, they cultivate colonies in their fur. To eat, the crabs simply comb their fur with their legs, and swallow a mouthful of microbial food.

Yeti crabs are blind, but they can sense temperature and crawl close to the scorching vent chimneys to make sure their bacteria have plenty of chemicals to grow. The males get closest of all, which is why they grow so big, but they do occasionally get boiled. Female crabs know the vent chimneys are not a safe place to be while they're brooding clutches of eggs stuck to their bellies. They creep away to find cooler water with more oxygen, but no bacteria grow in their fur, so slowly the females starve.

Several more species of yeti crab have been found around the world. In deep waters off Costa Rica, in a cooler environment called a cold seep, where methane bubbles through the seabed, there are yetis that dance. The crabs stir the water rhythmically with their claws, presumably to ensure a good supply of dissolved methane to feed their bacterial colonies. Near Antarctica in the Southern Ocean, there are white crabs that don't have hairy arms but instead hairy chests. In naming these ones, scientists took inspiration from David Hasselhoff and his role as a Los Angeles lifeguard in the 1990s American television series *Baywatch*, in which he wore red shorts and showed off his fine hairy chest. That species has come to be known, unofficially, as the Hoff crab.

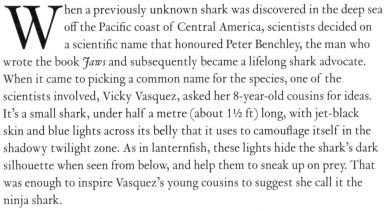

Ninja Lanternshark

Etmopterus benchleyi

When a previously unknown shark was discovered in the deep sea off the Pacific coast of Central America, scientists decided on a scientific name that honoured Peter Benchley, the man who wrote the book *Jaws* and subsequently became a lifelong shark advocate. When it came to picking a common name for the species, one of the scientists involved, Vicky Vasquez, asked her 8-year-old cousins for ideas. It's a small shark, under half a metre (about 1½ ft) long, with jet-black skin and blue lights across its belly that it uses to camouflage itself in the shadowy twilight zone. As in lanternfish, these lights hide the shark's dark silhouette when seen from below, and help them to sneak up on prey. That was enough to inspire Vasquez's young cousins to suggest she call it the ninja shark.

This is one of more than 40 lanternshark species, all of them deep-sea dwellers and many with interesting names. There are splendid lanternsharks, Marsha's and Laila's lanternsharks, blurred, pink and bristled lanternsharks (*Etmopterus splendidus*, *E. marshae*, *E. lailae*, *E. bigelowi*, *E. dianthus* and *E. unicolor*). The velvet belly lanternsharks (*E. spinax*) have glowing spines on their backs, which light up like a light sabre, warning off predators that will see the spines from a few metres away. The lanternsharks' main prey, pearlside fish (*Maurolicus* spp.), have poorer vision than their predators and probably see the spines only from nearby, when it's already too late and the lanternshark is swooping in for the kill.

Similar to the lanternsharks, another family of glowing deep-sea sharks are the kitefins (Dalatiidae). Among them are cookie-cutter sharks (*Isistius brasiliensis*), parasites that feed on large marine animals – including dolphins, whales, seals, tunas and bigger sharks – by biting a neat circular chunk of flesh from them, then swimming off. Cookie-cutter sharks are bioluminescent except for a band around their necks, which some scientists think may resemble the dark outline of small fish, luring in bigger predators by making them think there's something to eat. Pocket sharks (*Mollisquama parini*) are so named because they have a little pocket behind each pectoral fin, which contains bioluminescent slime. Nobody yet knows why the sharks have these pockets of glowing goo, but it's probably some kind of defence.

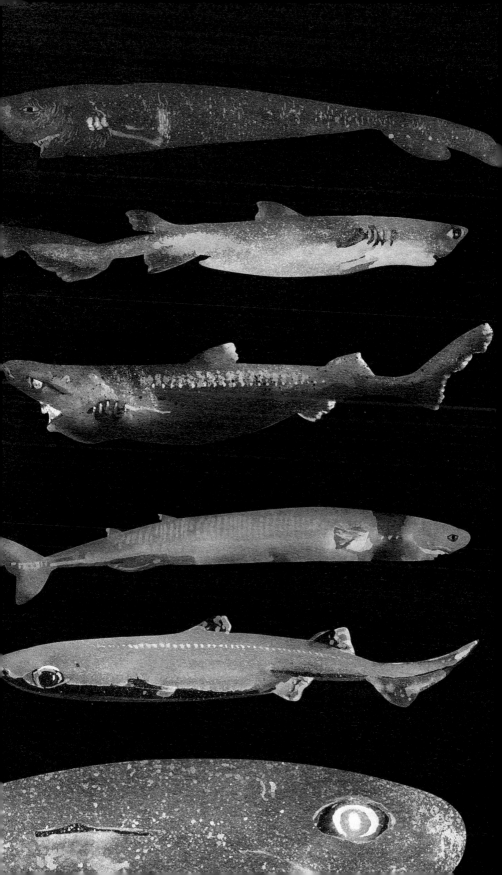

PACIFIC

Mariana Snailfish

Pseudoliparis swirei

Despite looking like giant tadpoles and being named after molluscs, snailfish are in fact fish. Their name comes from members of the snailfish family (the Liparidae) that live in coastal tide pools and kelp forests, and sucker themselves on to surfaces with their pelvic fins, rather like a snail does with its muscly, gluey foot. They are a curious bunch that have come to inhabit a wide range of habitats. There are snailfish that live in Arctic and Antarctic seas where to survive they've evolved antifreeze molecules in their bodies. Other snailfish live exclusively inside the gill chambers of king crabs. Most remarkable are the snailfish that live deeper in the ocean than any other fish.

Across the ocean there are about 27 oceanic trenches. These V-shaped chasms plunge downwards from the abyssal sea floor, collectively creating the ocean's lowest realm, called the hadal zone after Hades, the ancient Greek god of the underworld. A string of trenches in the western Pacific reach past the 10,000-metre (32,800 ft) mark. Deepest of all is the Mariana Trench, which is just shy of 11 kilometres (6¾ miles) deep – so deep that it could hide Mount Everest and seven Eiffel Towers stacked up. And it is home to the eponymous snailfish.

Other trenches have one or two of their own hadal snailfish. So far, at least 15 species have been found, some blue, some purple, some ghostly white. Most of what's known about them comes from remote cameras with bait attached, dropped by scientists into trenches and programmed to release from the sea floor after a day or so and float back up to the surface. The bait, usually mackerel, isn't to feed the snailfish but to attract scavenging crustaceans called amphipods, the snailfish's staple diet. Snailfish have tiny eyes and are probably blind, but they sense fidgeting amphipods from the ripples they send through the water. A snailfish's dimpled lips are full of nerve endings, and at the back of the throat is a second set of jaws, the pharyngeal jaws, that are perfect for crunching amphipods.

Snailfish survive in these trenches at crushing pressures, with the weight of an African elephant pressing down on every square inch (6.5 square centimetres) of their body. They are so well adapted to high pressure that when these pudgy fish are brought up to the surface they simply melt away. Their tissues are loaded with pressure-proof chemicals

134

that protect their cells and molecules so they can keep functioning and don't get bent out of shape.

It should come as no great surprise that a huge amount remains mysterious and unknown about hadal snailfish. Nobody knows where or how they breed. Do they stay in their trenches throughout their lives, or do they ever venture out? And how many more snailfish are still hiding in unexplored trenches?

Black-Lip Pearl Oyster

Pinctada margaritifera

Of all the many thousands of mollusc species in the world, oysters are widely considered to be the most elegant – at least, parts of them are. People have adored pearls for millennia, and have come up with various stories to explain their origins. It has been said that they are the tears of angels or deities, or that they form when lightning strikes an oyster, or that they grow from droplets of dew. The truth of the matter is that oysters are simply defending themselves. They create pearls as a form of immune response to deal with unwanted invaders in the form of parasites or grit, sand and chips of shell that irritate their soft insides. The oyster smothers these sharp fragments in thin, shiny layers of nacre, or mother-of-pearl, transforming them into smooth, harmless orbs.

All species of oyster, and other molluscs too, make pearls, but people have come to adore those from a few species, in particular black-lip pearl oysters, which produce dark, silvery pearls. Divers used to swim down and gather pearl oysters by hand from the sea, then open them up to search for rare, natural pearls. The industry is now dominated by farms where people have perfected the skill of inserting fragments into oysters and waiting a few years for the pearls to form.

It was only recently, however, that scientists unlocked the long-held secret of how oysters make such perfect, spherical pearls. A team of researchers took on the gruelling task of cutting through pearls and measuring the thickness of thousands of layers in each one. They saw that the layers follow the rules of a phenomenon called pink noise, in which events that appear random are in fact connected. Pink noise crops up everywhere, from earthquakes and classical music to brain activity and heartbeats. Inside an oyster, as each new layer of mother-of-pearl is laid down, it adapts precisely to the one before. This constant adjustment means that any small imperfections aren't made worse but are smoothed out. The resulting pearls are not only beautiful and shiny, but also incredibly tough – 3,000 times tougher than the materials from which they're made, calcium carbonate and protein. Understanding how exactly pearls are made to be so strong could lead to a new generation of super-materials, for manufacturing devices such as solar panels and spacecraft.

Mother-of-pearl also lines the inside of many mollusc shells, giving them a crack-proof covering that can survive the crushing attack of crab claws and fish jaws. This too is a material that people have traditionally used, to make fishhooks, tools, jewellery and ornaments. Circles cut from black-lipped oyster shells have widely been used as shirt buttons, as have those from gold-lipped oysters (*Pinctada maxima*), abalone (*Haliotis* spp.) and freshwater pearl mussels (*Margaritifera margaritifera*). Biotech companies are now looking into mother-of-pearl to find the next big biomedical breakthroughs. Mother-of-pearl could be used as a new form of dental filling and a new kind of bone graft to help broken bones heal.

Pearl oysters are not, strictly speaking, what scientists consider to be true oysters, which belong to a different family (Ostreidae). Among the true oysters are cockscomb oysters (*Lopha cristagalli*) with their distinctive zigzag shapes that inspired the form of the Sydney Opera House. There are also culinary favourites, the Pacific oysters, Sydney rock oysters and Olympia oysters (*Magallana gigas*, *Saccostrea glomerata* and *Ostrea lurida* respectively). Various oyster species grow naturally in huge aggregations, but these reefs have suffered terribly from habitat destruction. New York, for instance, was once the world's oyster capital, surrounded by reefs covering an area ten times bigger than Manhattan. Dredging, pollution and over-fishing all took their toll, and the last New York oysters were shucked and slurped in the early twentieth century. Efforts are now underway to restore those lost oyster reefs, and there are similar projects around the world.

Pompeii Worm

Alvinella pompejana

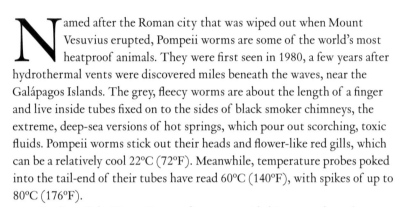

Named after the Roman city that was wiped out when Mount Vesuvius erupted, Pompeii worms are some of the world's most heatproof animals. They were first seen in 1980, a few years after hydrothermal vents were discovered miles beneath the waves, near the Galápagos Islands. The grey, fleecy worms are about the length of a finger and live inside tubes fixed on to the sides of black smoker chimneys, the extreme, deep-sea versions of hot springs, which pour out scorching, toxic fluids. Pompeii worms stick out their heads and flower-like red gills, which can be a relatively cool 22°C (72°F). Meanwhile, temperature probes poked into the tail-end of their tubes have read 60°C (140°F), with spikes of up to 80°C (176°F).

Studies of the Pompeii worms' genes provide hints as to how they avoid being boiled alive. They make heat-shock proteins that don't break down in the immense heat, and a tough form of collagen (an important molecule that builds many parts of living bodies) that tolerates the extreme heat and pressure. The fuzzy grey coat is made of microbes that may help to detoxify the noxious fluids that flow out of vent chimneys.

Other microbes living on hydrothermal vents survive even higher temperatures. Hyperthermophiles don't just tolerate extreme heat – they love it, and grow best when their surroundings are 80°C (176°F) or hotter. These microbes that keep working at such high temperatures have become incredibly important in the human world.

If you've taken a test for COVID-19 that was sent off to a lab, there's a good chance it involved a molecule that was originally discovered on hydrothermal vents. PCR or Polymerase Chain Reaction tests involve snipping samples of DNA into pieces and making millions of copies, which scientists then sequence to identify if any coronavirus DNA is present. The same tests are used in DNA fingerprinting and all sorts of other genetic analysis. Copies of the DNA snippets are made using enzymes called polymerases that were originally discovered in microbes in hot springs in Yellowstone National Park. Versions of these enzymes from hydrothermal vents work even better and more accurately at the high temperatures at which these tests must be conducted.

Smooth Handfish

Sympterichthys unipennis

The smooth handfish from Tasmania holds the unfortunate record of being the first fish in modern times to be declared extinct. That happened in March 2020, although 18 months later it was announced as being non-extinct – maybe. The reversal happened because experts decided that people looking for handfish hadn't checked everywhere the species might be hiding out. It's a lot easier to prove that a species still exists than it is to be absolutely sure it doesn't. Maybe smooth handfish are still hanging on somewhere, but nobody has reported seeing one for more than 200 years. The species probably disappeared because dredging for oysters and scallops in the nineteenth and twentieth centuries destroyed the shellfish reefs where they lived. Smooth handfish probably became extinct decades ago and no one noticed at the time.

There are 13 other species of handfish living today in waters off southeast Australia and around Tasmania. They belong to a small family of anglerfish, the Brachionichthyidae, a portmanteau of the Latin word *bracchium* (arm) and the Greek *ichthys* (fish). These little fish do indeed look as though they have arms, hands and fingers – all fashioned from their pectoral fins – and they walk slowly across the seabed. The rest of the time they just sit there. Even when they're young, handfish are not great travellers. There's no drifting larval stage in their life cycle, so they don't disperse far. This makes them highly likely to be snagged in fishing nets and renders them prone to habitat damage and the accelerating threat of climate change. Sea temperatures around Tasmania are rising about four times faster than the global average. Immobile species that prefer cooler waters, such as handfish, have no way to escape.

There is some good news, however. In 2021 scientists lowered a camera on to the seabed 150 metres (490 ft) down, in a marine reserve off Tasmania. Watching the footage later, one of them spotted a small pink fish of a kind that nobody had seen in 22 years. It was a pink handfish (*Brachiopsilus dianthus*). Until then, scientists thought the species lived only in shallow, sheltered bays. So perhaps there are more handfish hiding in the deep.

Sunflower Sea Star

Pycnopodia helianthoides

Sunflower sea stars are big and beautiful. They can be yellow and orange, purple and red. Their 24 arms can stretch across a metre (3 ft), the size of a tractor wheel, making them one of the world's largest starfish, although of course they're not really fish. To avoid confusion, some marine biologists insist we call them all sea stars instead. Together with sea cucumbers and sea urchins, brittlestars and feather stars, the sea stars formerly known as starfish belong to a group of spiny-skinned animals called echinoderms.

These are benthic animals, the kind that spend their lives on the seabed. But sunflower sea stars are not as dozy as they may at first appear. They scuttle about on thousands of tiny tube feet, which carry them along at impressive speeds of a metre (3 ft) a minute. They eat clams, sea snails and dead squid as well as other echinoderms, especially sea urchins – one reason they are very much missed now that so many of them are gone.

In 2013 a terrible plague struck the western coast of North America that devastated many species of sea stars. It was a gruesome sight. Lesions covered sea stars' skin, their legs dropped off, and within a few days the stricken animals melted into a pile of slime. Sunflower sea stars used to be common between Alaska and Mexico, but now they are missing from most of their range. Scientists estimate that almost 6 billion of them died. It's a disaster not only for the sea stars but also for whole ecosystems. The collapse coincided with the loss of many kelp forests, which were wiped out by heatwaves, and a boom in purple sea urchins (*Strongylocentrotus purpuratus*). Without sea stars to keep their numbers in check, sea urchins are thriving, and their intensive grazing is stopping kelp sporelings from settling and growing.

Marine biologists are still not exactly sure what happened to the sea stars. The cause of sea star wasting syndrome, as it's come to be known, has proven difficult to identify. At first people thought it might have been triggered by a virus. Later studies suggest other microbes are involved, that suck oxygen out of the water, essentially suffocating the sea stars. The climate crisis and heatwaves are also implicated in the complex picture of the changing ocean.

There are glimmers of hope, though. Small clusters of sea stars are surviving in cooler waters and could help the rest of the population recover.

And in 2021 scientists worked out for the first time how to breed sunflower sea stars in captivity. Not everyone thinks it will come to this, but maybe one day it will be possible to release them back into the wild.

Nudibranch

Nudibranchia

Nudibranchs, otherwise known as sea slugs, are phenomenally more beautiful than their terrestrial counterparts. Thousands of species are decorated in rainbow colours and patterns, and not just tropical seas but also cooler waters are home to all sorts of stunning sea slugs. For some, their bright colours are camouflage. Banana-yellow sea slugs, for example, live and feed on yellow sponges. For others, the colours are a warning to would-be predators that these soft-bodied, shell-less molluscs are not good to eat. Many sea slugs are laced with bad-tasting chemicals. This is why swimming sea slugs, known as sea angels, are kidnapped by little crustaceans called amphipods, which carry them around as if they were a backpack. Fish and other predators know to leave the amphipod alone or risk a revolting mouthful of noxious sea angel.

One particular species of sea slug, *Jorunna parva*, became an internet sensation. Nicknamed sea bunnies, they're fuzzy and white with a pair of fluffy 'ears' that are in fact sensory organs called rhinophores that detect chemicals in the water. Their 'tails' are actually their gills, which poke out as they do in all nudibranchs ('nudibranch' means naked gill). As well as nudibranchs, an assortment of other gastropods go by the name sea slug, including plakobranchs and pteropods. Their collective feature is a lack of external shell.

Among them, sea slugs perform a variety of unique tricks. Several are kleptomaniacs. Leaf sheep (*Costasiella kuroshimae*) are bright-green sea slugs that graze on algae and in doing so become solar-powered. They keep the algae's chloroplasts, the tiny structures that soak up the sun's energy to make food, and put them in their skin, where they continue to photosynthesize. This means that when there's not a lot of algae around to eat, leaf sheep can simply bask in the sun, drawing on their inbuilt food factories. In a similar way, but this time for defence, sea swallows (*Glaucus atlanticus*) steal the stinging cells from the Portuguese man o' war they feed on. These striking blue sea slugs push the intact stingers into their finger-like projections, called cerata.

Sea slugs have remarkable abilities to regrow parts of their bodies. One species (*Chromodoris reticulata*) has a disposable penis that drops off after it mates, then regrows within 24 hours. Another (*Elysia marginata*) has the rather more alarming trick of ripping off its head. The decapitated head wanders around on its own for a while and eventually grows a whole new body (the abandoned body lives on for only a few days, and doesn't grow a new head). It's possible the sea slug does this to rid itself of a body that's become infested with parasites.

Besides revealing many of the intricate wonders of nature, sea slugs have also taught us a lot about human brains. Since the 1960s, the neuroscientist Eric Kandel has been studying a type of sea slug called the California sea hare (*Aplysia californica*) to try to find out how memories are made. He picked sea hares because they have large nerve cells that can be seen even without a microscope. There are also not too many of them: about 20,000, compared to 100 billion neurons in humans. Even with this simple nervous system, sea hares learn and remember things. Gently prod one and it retracts its external gill and siphon. Over time, sea hares learn to respond differently to different stimuli. Kandel watched how individual sea-hare nerves changed as memories formed. He saw that short-term memories lead to temporary changes in the connections between nerves. Long-term memories, on the other hand, cause lasting anatomical changes in the brain. What's true in these molluscs is also true in humans. In 2000 Kandel shared a Nobel Prize for his work understanding memory formation, as inspired by sea hares.

In 2021 another team of scientists figured that Artificial Intelligence could get smarter by becoming more like sea slugs. Two key signs of intelligence in the simple minds of sea hares are habituation (becoming used to a stimulus over time) and sensitization (reacting more strongly to a new stimulus). At the moment AI is not very good at remembering new, important things while forgetting things that don't matter as much. The scientists managed to get a quantum material to behave in a similar way to sea slugs, via habituation and sensitization, a first step towards making better self-driving cars and those all-important social-media algorithms.

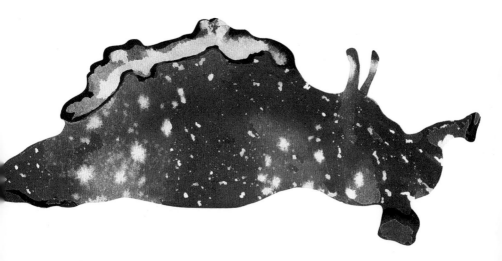

Pacific Dragonfish

Idiacanthus antrostomus

In the waters of the twilight zone, hundreds of metres beneath the surface of the sea, there are fish that are blacker than the sunless ocean itself. Scientists have long known that many deep-sea fish are extremely black. For one thing, they're difficult to photograph; even with several flashlights trained on them, they appear in photographs as a featureless black outline, and their skin sucks in light like a miniature black hole. It is only recently, though, that scientists have discovered just how these animals go about making themselves so black.

Their skin contains structures filled with melanin, the pigment that is found in the skin of humans and other animals, only much more densely packed. The melanin granules in the skin of deep-sea fish are arranged in such a way as to trap photons. Imagine a pinball machine with a ball pinging around inside between the flippers and bumpers; the same kind of thing happens to light pinging between melanin granules. Light enters the skin and bounces sideways, and almost none is reflected out again.

A sheet of black construction paper absorbs about 90 per cent of the light that falls on it, and a new car tyre about 99 per cent. Many deep-sea fish absorb 99.95 per cent of the light that hits their skin. This is around the same absorbency as the blackest human-engineered material, Vantablack, which is made from carbon nanotubes. This discovery in fish has got material scientists excited because it shows a new and potentially much more efficient way of making ultra-black materials that have various uses, such as lining high-powered telescopes.

For other animals, such as butterflies and birds of paradise, ultra-dark coloration offsets their brighter pigments, making them look more eye-catching to potential mates. For deep-sea fish, being black is all about not being seen – in particular by their own light. Pacific dragonfish, in common with many deep-sea fish, are bioluminescent. They have a long barbel dangling from their chin with a glowing tip that lures in prey. It's likely that dragonfish evolved their black skin to avoid reflecting their own glowing lights, since the lure wouldn't work if the prey spotted the predator with a huge gaping mouth. Dragonfish teeth are also structured to avoid twinkling in their own light.

Besides black skin and non-glinting teeth, deep-sea fish have evolved a range of features that help them to cope in the extreme conditions of the deep. Many of these are what make deep-sea fish look so weird, but it's all about survival. A major challenge is finding enough to eat. Various predatory fish have a mouth and stomach big enough to gulp down whatever prey they happen to come across, no matter how big. Black swallowers (*Chiasmodon niger*) have a massively distensible stomach that lets them swallow fish that are more than twice their size. Pelican eels (*Eurypharynx pelecanoides*) and gulper eels (*Saccopharynx* spp.) have enormous mouths that occupy up to a quarter of their body length and open out like umbrellas. Goblin sharks (*Mitsukurina owstoni*) swing open their jaws to a record-breaking 116 degrees and sling them forwards by half a head length, then snap them shut in less than half a second.

Tripodfish, also known as spiderfish (*Bathypterois* spp.), spend much of their time perched high above the seabed on the extended lower tip of their tail and two elongated pelvic fins, which can be three times as long as their body. Sitting still in this way hoists them up into the current, where they use their long, sensitive pectoral fins to detect planktonic prey wafting by.

Other odd-looking but important adaptations of many deep-sea fish are their eyes, which have evolved to be super sensitive. Pacific barreleyes (*Macropinna microstoma*), tube-eyes (*Stylephorus chordatus*) and others have huge cylindrical eyes that help them detect dim traces of light.

Vampire Squid

Vampyroteuthis infernalis

The vampire squid appears at first to be a terrifying beast. It has velvety, blood-red skin, a snapping white beak and webbed arms covered in sharp-looking spikes. In fact, these are gentle creatures and quite small, reaching the size of a rugby ball. They inhabit the deep sea, hundreds of metres down, and feed on fluffy white particles of organic matter that sink from above, known as marine snow (this stuff sounds nice, but it is mostly dead plankton and their faeces that clump together and drift downwards). Vampire squid catch snow by unfurling a long filament, eight times their body length, on to which the flakes of marine snow settle. Then they slowly reel in their filaments, scrape up the snowy particles, pack them into snowballs and swallow them.

The species was first discovered in the Atlantic at the end of the nineteenth century by the German zoologist Carl Chun, during the Valdivia Expedition, which set out to prove that life exists in the ocean deeper than the first 300 fathoms, or 550 metres (1,805 ft). As the vampire squid and many other collected specimens showed, life does indeed descend far beneath the waves.

Originally thought to be an octopus, vampire squid are in fact a relict group, part way between squid and octopuses. Various extinct vampyromorphids have been found as fossils, but *Vampyroteuthis infernalis* is the only living species.

The vampires are harmless, but for a genuinely terrifying squid look no further than the Humboldt squid (*Dosidicus gigas*). Mexican fishermen call them *diabolo rojo*, red devils, and for good reason. They're typically 1.5 metres (5 ft) long, making them the third-largest squid (after giant and colossal squid), with deep-red skin and a reputation as aggressive predators. They hunt at night in coordinated shoals, swimming up from the deep sea in spirals towards the surface as they chase lanternfish and other squid. They'll eat each other given a chance, and have been known to attack scuba divers. Recent studies suggest that Humboldt squid may communicate with each other and coordinate their hunts using patterns flickering across their bodies. They can also make their skin glow, illuminating their messages in the dark.

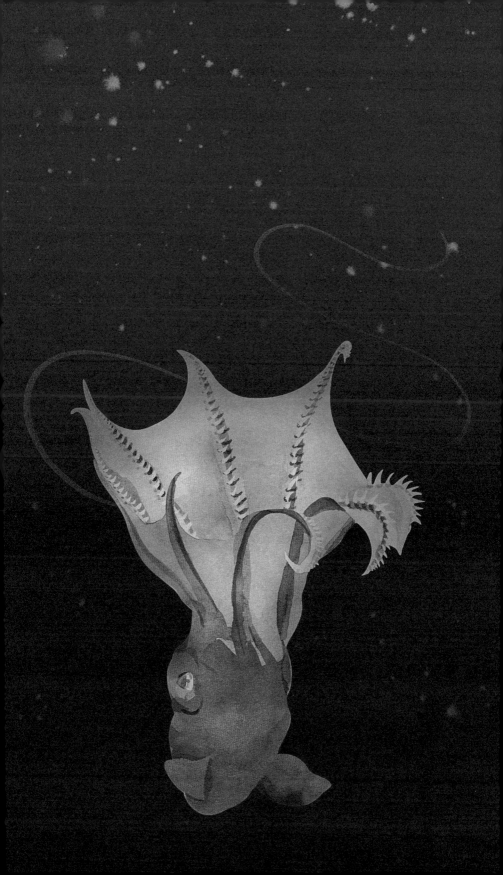

Eyelash Harptail Blenny

Meiacanthus atrodorsalis

Little fish called eyelash harptail blennies get their name from their appearance: an elegant black eye-line leading back from each eye, and a crescent or harp-shaped tail. They are members of a group that also goes by two other descriptive names, the sabretooth or fangblennies. Despite their diminutive stature, fangblennies are fearless as they swim around their coral-reef homes safe in the knowledge that they are packing a powerful weapon in their mouths. They constitute one of only two groups of fish (the other is the little-known deep-sea eels) that have venomous bites. If a large predator tries to swallow one, chances are it will quickly spit the fangblenny right back out again.

Fish are the most venomous vertebrates. Close to 3,000 known species produce venom – far more than venomous snake species – although most deliver their venom in spines on their bodies rather than through their teeth. Like their ability to generate electric shocks, venoms have evolved repeatedly among the fish, at least 18 times independently, including in lionfish (*Pterois* spp.), stonefish (*Synanceia*) and weeverfish (Trachinidae), which are commonly trodden on by European beachgoers and deliver excruciating stings. Fish are only defending themselves; they don't use venom to hunt prey.

Scientists have found that fangblennies make a mixture of chemicals in their venom glands and inject them through hollow teeth. One is a type commonly found in scorpions, bees and snakes, which damages nerves and causes inflammation. Another is a toxin also found in cone snails that causes a victim's blood pressure to crash and makes them feel dizzy.

Various impersonators lurk among the fangblennies. Blue-striped fangblennies (*Plagiotremus rhinorhynchos*) hang around at cleaning stations on coral reefs pretending to be young bluestreak cleaner wrasse (*Labroides dimidiatus*). They look so similar to genuine cleaners that the fangblennies go undetected and get away with cheating. Instead of offering an honest cleaning service, picking off parasites and dead skin, the fangblennies chomp the client fish's living tissue, perhaps sedating them as they do with a dose of numbing venom. Various harmless fish have also evolved to look like fangblennies, gaining protection from their fearsome reputation without going to the trouble of making their own venom.

CARIBBEAN

Lionfish

Pterois spp.

Lionfish look like the kind of fish you should leave well alone. Bold red-and-white stripes and long, fluttering spines give the distinct impression of a formidable animal – which is precisely the idea. Those spines deliver an excruciating and potentially lethal sting, and the bright colours are a warning sign that in recent years have been spreading around the world.

Two species, the red lionfish (*Pterois volitans*) and the devil firefish (*P. miles*), are native to coral reefs in the Pacific and Indian oceans respectively. In the 1980s, however, they were spotted off the coast of Florida. Most probably they were released from home aquariums, either accidentally or on purpose (nobody has owned up). Possibly as few as 12 fish were originally set free, but soon there were many more. By the 2000s, lionfish were making their way south, into the Gulf of Mexico and the coral reefs of the Caribbean. By 2014 they had made it all the way to Brazil.

People move all sorts of wild species around the world, but we generally hear only about the ones that escape into the wild, proliferate and make a nuisance of themselves. Lionfish happen to have a suite of troublemaking traits, not least their huge fecundity. By their first birthday, they can spawn every two to four days. A female releases two million eggs a year, in floating clumps that can drift for hundreds or thousands of miles before hatching.

Young lionfish grow quickly into skilful ambush predators, and when they end up a long way from home, they find it very easy to hunt. Caribbean fish, especially young ones, don't see the foreign lionfish as a threat and have no instinct to swim away. Some even swim towards a lionfish and hide among their long spines, mistaking them for corals to shelter in. As a consequence, lionfish across the Caribbean are gorging themselves silly. Scientists have found some with fatty liver disease, a fish version of gout normally seen only in overfed pet fish.

To make matters worse, lionfish have few native predators in their new ranges. Sharks and groupers don't recognize them as potential food. The upshot is that when lionfish arrive, their numbers explode and populations of native fish tend to plummet.

More recently, lionfish have begun to show up in the Mediterranean Sea, among hundreds of Red Sea species that migrated along the Suez

154

Canal. In the past, cooler Mediterranean temperatures kept tropical species at bay, but as the seas warm many are expanding their ranges. Lionfish were first seen off Israel in 1991, although they didn't survive (perhaps owing to the winter cold), and it was another 20 years before the species started to spread. They now live in Lebanon, Syria, Turkey, Greece and Cyprus, and they're moving into the Ionian and Aegean seas.

As lionfish have spread, so have efforts to curb their numbers. Most experts agree there's probably no getting rid of lionfish once they've taken hold somewhere. Nevertheless, their impact on local ecosystems can be reduced by adopting a rather unusual approach to marine conservation: to catch and eat as many fish as possible. Lionfish derbies offer prizes to spear fishers who catch the biggest, the smallest and the most lionfish in a day. It's tough luck for the lionfish, who through no fault of their own have ended up in unwanted places, but none of them needs go to waste. A lionfish's venomous spines can easily be cut off, their venom is deactivated by cooking and, most importantly, their meat tastes good. People have also begun to make jewellery out of lionfish fins, and leather from their skin.

In parts of the Caribbean where lionfish first invaded, things are starting to look up and lionfish numbers are declining, perhaps from targeted fishing. This offers hope that in some places the worst of the invasion could be over.

Goliath Grouper

Epinephelus itajara

As the name suggests, goliath groupers are very big fish. Fully grown adults can measure 2.5 metres (just over 8 ft) from nose to tail and weigh close to half a tonne – similar to a good-sized grizzly bear. A goliath can swallow a metre-long (3 ft) shark in a single gulp. And they have one of the loudest, deepest voices of any fish. Scuba divers in the vicinity of a goliath grouper might feel their insides shaking as the fish's sonic boom pulses through the water. Most likely, the male groupers are vying for territory and females.

Such big fish have, unsurprisingly, been a tempting target for fishermen, and there have been commercial fisheries in the past. Goliath grouper meat was canned for dog food and their carcasses stuffed full of drugs to smuggle them into the United States. Mostly, though, goliath groupers have been hunted by sports fishers. Just as there are trophy hunters who like to kill large animals on land, such as lions and elephants, so there are their oceanic counterparts.

For decades, goliath groupers were a favourite of trophy hunters in Florida. Sometimes fishers would take their catches home to mount on a wall, but most often they just posed alongside their prize catches to snap a picture before throwing them back into the sea, already dead. Archives of sports fishers' photographs from Key West in Florida have documented the goliaths' historic decline. In the 1950s huge groupers, including goliaths, were the main species that sports fishers hooked. Big sharks were also popular, including hammerheads and great whites. Often the fish would outweigh the people onboard a sport fishing boat. By the late 1970s most of those big predatory fish had gone. Instead, sports fishers had to make do with smaller species such as snappers. Since the 1990s it's been illegal to catch and kill goliath groupers in Florida, and their numbers have been increasing slowly.

One of the goliath's close relatives, the Nassau grouper (*Epinephelus striatus*), has also suffered badly from over-fishing. Similar to humphead wrasse, Nassau groupers meet up in vast shoals to spawn at predictable times and places, making them an easy target for fishermen. Nassau groupers were the basis for the most important reef fisheries across the Caribbean until their spawning aggregations collapsed and populations were completely wiped out. But there are signs that even Nassau groupers can recover. In the Cayman Islands, science-based conservation measures have been introduced to help to bring the groupers back. Their spawning sites are strictly protected from fishing and there are limits on catch sizes and on the gear fishers can use. The upshot is that over 15 years, the population of Nassau groupers around Little Cayman has tripled to become the largest known population of this species anywhere in the world.

CARIBBEAN

Flying Fish

Exocoetidae

At the beginning of the twentieth century, around the time the Wright brothers emulated birds and took off in the first heavier-than-air powered flight, scientists also started looking to another type of flying animal for ideas of how to build aeroplanes. Flying fish are closer living analogies for aeroplanes than most birds because they don't flap their 'wings'. Biologists had argued over this detail for some time, because at the speed flying fish zip through the air, it's not easy to see whether they flutter or hold their wing-like fins still. But flying fish don't have big flight muscles as birds do, nor an attachment point on their skeleton. They glide. Among the 60 or so species of flying fish, some are 'monoplanes' and glide on a single pair of fins (pectorals), and some are 'biplanes', with two pairs of elongated fins (pectorals and pelvics). These weren't the inspiration for aeroplanes, but it's curious that fish and humans arrived at similar solutions to the challenge of flight.

The flights of flying fish generally last for less than a minute. They gather speed by sculling their tail from side to side, up to 70 times per second, then leap into the air, and they can glide for several hundred metres across the waves. Korean scientists recently tested dead, stuffed flying fish in a wind tunnel and found them to be as efficient at gliding as hawks.

Being a fish out of water has its advantages for flying fish. There were early ideas that it saved them energy, but it's more likely that they're escaping dolphins, dorado and other predators. Flying fish sometimes change direction while airborne to throw attackers off their trail.

Sushi connoisseurs will be familiar with the gleaming piles of orange flying-fish roe, or *tobiko*. Various countries harvest them, in particular Brazil, where fishers throw bundles of coconut palms into the sea. Female flying fish lay their eggs in the floating raft and the fishers pick them off by hand.

In Barbados, flying fish are highly prized. They're a key ingredient in the national dish *cou-cou*, and feature in passports and on dollar coins. There's also one flying fish that leapt clear of the ocean and into the southern night sky, as the constellation Volans.

VOLANS

Sea Cow

Sirenia

M any stories have been told of sea cows. A common one is that of Christopher Columbus spotting them in the Caribbean in 1472 and reporting that they were an ugly version of the beautiful mermaids he'd heard so much about. The scientific name for this group of gentle, herbivorous aquatic mammals is Sirenia, the sirens. Throughout their range the two groups of sea cows, the manatees and the dugongs, have stirred myths and embodied the humans, hybrids and deities who span land and water.

Dugongs (*Dugong dugon*) live along the coast of East Africa and across Asia, where people have known of them for millennia. Neolithic rock art in Gua Tambun, Malaysia, depicts a menagerie of animals including a deer, a tapir, turtles, a goat and a dugong. Various South East Asian folk tales tell of the origins of these mysterious, human-like dugongs, commonly involving women who fell into the water and sprouted a fish's tail. Connected to these stories, dugongs are revered in many places, and it's bad luck to kill one.

Elsewhere, dugongs have been traditionally hunted. From the Red Sea and the Arabian Gulf to northern Australia, dugongs used to be caught for their meat and oil. The Bajau Laut (sea nomads) around Borneo hunt dugongs silently at night using spears, and consider their meat a delicacy. In many cultures dugong bones, oil and meat are said to hold supernatural powers. In China they've been called 'miraculous fish' and their oil used as a traditional medicine, while in parts of Indonesia and Thailand dugong tears are considered an aphrodisiac. Across the Japanese island of Okinawa, dugong bones are found in ancient burial sites, carved into the shape of butterflies and coloured red with ochre. Archaeologists suggest that these were used in magical ceremonies, perhaps embodying the spirits that guided souls into the afterlife.

Three species of Sirenian live on either side of the Atlantic – the West African, West Indian and Amazonian manatees (*Trichechus senegalensis, T. manatus* and *T. inunguis*) – where there are similar traditional beliefs and uses as for dugongs. Nigerian myths warn that if you encounter a manatee in the water it will tickle you until you drown. Also in Nigeria, where manatee meat is used as a treatment for diabetes, the manatee's eyes are said to hold magic powers, and faeces found inside a manatee's stomach are used to mend broken bones.

In the East and West Atlantic, manatees have become entwined with tales of mermaids. The African water spirit Mami Wata is often depicted as a mermaid and sometimes associated with manatees. She can be seductive and dangerous, a protector, a healer and a bringer of riches. She is worshipped and celebrated in various forms across Africa, and was brought to the Americas with the transatlantic slave trade, where she took on the important role of protector of enslaved mothers and children. Over the centuries Mami Wata has shifted her identity, taking on elements of European mermaid legends, Hindu deities and Islamic saints, but she's still recognizable in contemporary art and artefacts.

Another species of Sirenian comes with its own, rather different kind of legend. Steller's sea cows (*Hydrodamalis gigas*) used to live in the cold waters of the Bering Sea, and at up to 10 metres (33 ft) long they were three times bigger than dugongs and manatees, and by far the biggest sirenians humans ever saw. These enormous, blubber-coated sea cows floated in the shallows, grazing on kelp and communicating with each other through snorts and sighs.

These sea cows were named after the German explorer, zoologist and botanist Georg Wilhelm Steller, who encountered them while shipwrecked in the Commander Islands, east of Kamchatka, Russia, in the 1740s. Subsequently, these docile creatures proved all too easy to kill. Reports describe hunters simply hauling them out of the water and leaving them stranded on beaches to expire under their colossal body weight. Sealers and fur traders killed them for their fat and meat, which is said to have tasted like corned beef. By the end of the eighteenth century the last of the giant sea cows had died and the species became extinct. Recent analysis of DNA extracted from the bones of Steller's sea cows suggests that they may have been on their way out long before Palaeolithic and then modern humans started hunting them. Sea cows used to live across the northern Pacific, from Japan to California, but climate change over tens of thousands of years pushed them into a spiralling decline from which they never recovered.

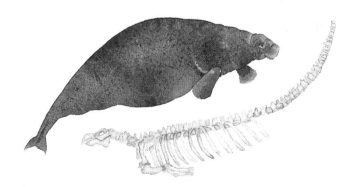

Lemon Shark

Negaprion brevirostris

More is known about the lives of lemon sharks than about probably any other large shark species, and they're helping to shift lingering misconceptions about these toothy predators. Sharks are not mindless killing machines, as many people might once have assumed, but thoughtful animals with personalities, which are capable of learning and remembering.

Eugenie Clark, the Shark Lady, as she came to be known, was a pioneering scientist who first started working with lemon sharks and showed the public that sharks were deeply misunderstood. In the 1950s she conducted studies with lemon sharks in sea pens at her research facility in Florida. She showed that, just like other animals, such as dogs, lemon sharks could be trained with food to do things. Her sharks learned to press a striped underwater target with their noses, triggering a bell and rewarding them with a piece of fish. It wasn't quite the shark equivalent of Pavlov's dogs, and Clark didn't look to see if the sharks salivated at the sound of a bell, but they quickly learned what they needed to do to get food. The tests also showed that the sharks could remember the trick for at least a few months. Over winter, the water temperature dropped and the sharks stopped feeding. Then, as the sea warmed up in spring, Clark lowered the target back into the water and the sharks still knew exactly what to do.

More of the lemon shark's secrets are coming to light in the Bahamas, where a research station dedicated to sharks has been running since 1990. In the mangrove forests of Bimini Island, young lemon sharks spend their first three years hiding among submerged roots and trunks, out of sight of bigger predators, while they learn how to hunt and survive. At certain times of day they emerge from the mangroves and roam the sandy seabed, where their yellowish tint (hence their name) may help to camouflage them.

Studies around Bimini have shown that juvenile sharks tend to hang out in gangs. They prefer to swim with sharks they already know, rather than with strangers. Within the gangs, there are sharks with different personalities. Some are bold and like to lead, while others are consistently content with following the others around. A similar thing happens among lemon sharks kept in large aquarium tanks. It's not known whether they're making friends exactly, but lemon sharks do learn more quickly from each other when they're part of a well-established social network.

Closely related sharks from the Indo-Pacific, the sickle-fin lemon sharks, perform a type of body language. In French Polynesia, scientists set up a camera around a box of bait and filmed as the sharks took turns to feed. To their surprise, it wasn't the biggest sharks that got first dibs on the food, but the boldest. Those at the top of the pecking order asserted their dominance by swimming aggressively towards their rivals. Lower-ranking sharks always turned away and behaved submissively.

Back in Bimini, a 30-year study has uncovered another aspect to the lemon sharks' complex lives. Young adult sharks were fitted with satellite tags, and scientists tracked them as they left their gangs in the mangroves and set off on long migrations over thousands of kilometres. For more than a decade that generation of sharks stayed away from the Bimini mangroves, until eventually the females began to come back. It turns out that when the time comes for them to have their own pups, female lemon sharks return to the place where they were born. This puts lemon sharks alongside salmon, sea turtles and other great ocean navigators that find their way back to their natal grounds. How lemon sharks navigate is another mystery that has yet to be solved, although it may be that their electrosensitive snouts detect the Earth's geomagnetic field and draw a map in their minds.

Pufferfish

Tetraodontiformes

Pufferfish are famous for two things: their amazing ability to inflate, and the fact that eating one can easily kill you.

The story used to go that when pufferfish get scared they swim up to the surface of the sea and suck in air. Then they bob about like a beach ball, out of reach of the jaws of underwater predators. In fact, an alarmed pufferfish stays where it is and swallows seawater, filling a pouch in its stomach that has folded sides and expands like an accordion until its body is up to three times the original volume. The effect is not to float but to suddenly become a big ball that's too cumbersome for an attacker to grab. This anatomical feat of hyperinflation is possible because a pufferfish's skin is eight times stretchier than that of most fish. They also have no ribs or pelvic bone that would get in the way. Porcupinefish are related to pufferfish and have spines that stand on end when they puff, turning them into a prickly nuisance.

If a predator somehow defeats a pufferfish's first line of defence and manages to take a bite, another nasty surprise awaits them. Many parts of a pufferfish, including the skin, intestines and, most of all, the liver, are spiked with a potent neurotoxin called tetrodotoxin, or TTX. This chemical is hundreds of times more lethal than cyanide. TTX is also what gives blue-ringed octopuses their deadly bite and makes various newts, toads and sea slugs extremely dangerous to eat. It works by blocking nerve signals, and causes paralysis and eventually death by suffocation. There's no known antidote.

Pufferfish don't poison themselves because they have a genetic mutation that stops TTX from binding to their nerve fibres. Even though humans are not at all resistant to the toxin, they have been eating them – very carefully – for a long time. Ancient middens in Japan dating back to the Jōmon period, as much as 5,000 years ago, contain not only discarded clam shells but also pufferfish bones. Still popular today, chefs train for several years to get a *fugu*-handling licence and learn the skills of extracting the liver so their dishes aren't lethal.

Pufferfish obtain TTX from bacteria in their food. It's now possible to rear toxin-free pufferfish in captivity and exclude the bacteria from their diet, making them perfectly safe to eat. However, demand continues for the wild-caught variety from diehard *fugu* fans.

In the Caribbean, extract of pufferfish has been associated with a rather shadier recipe. Priests of the African diasporic vodou religion, known in the West as voodoo, have gained notoriety for their ability to turn people into zombies. Potions made from the ground-up pieces of various noxious animals, including pufferfish, are said to have the power to convince people they have died and come back as the living dead. Exactly what role the pufferfish extract and TTX have to play in all this remains murky.

Close relatives of pufferfish include triggerfish, whose name comes from the sharp spine on their backs, which is released by a trigger mechanism. They use it to wedge themselves into crevices on a coral reef so that predators can't pull them out. Boxfish, as their name suggests, are encased in a bony box. When alarmed, they exude into the water a noxious slime. Sunfish are cousins of pufferfish that approach the business of defending themselves by simply being much bigger than almost anything else.

While pufferfish and their relatives seem preoccupied by defence, there is also great beauty to be found among these species. Many pufferfish, triggerfish, cowfish and trunkfish have intricate patterns and iridescent colours. Some species are also talented artists. In the seas surrounding the Amami archipelago in Japan, mysterious circles 2 metres (6½ ft) across appeared on the sandy seabed like underwater crop circles. People puzzled over them for a long while until eventually, in 2011, scuba divers saw a white-spotted pufferfish drawing in the sand.

A male pufferfish toils over his artwork for at least a week. He swims over the seabed, fanning the sand with his fins and sculpting a circle, then decorating it with seashells and pieces of coral. His goal is to attract the attention of a female who he hopes will come along and lay her eggs in the exquisite nest. Then the male pufferfish watches over the eggs until they hatch.

CARIBBEAN

Damselfish

Pomacentridae

D
amselfish are only small – most species are palm-sized – but you'd
think they weren't aware of their diminutive stature if you saw
how some of them behave. On coral reefs, they chase much bigger
fish and even accost scuba divers, darting angrily at their masks. But these
harmless herbivores won't hurt you; they're just defending their territory.
Damselfish are one of the few non-human animals – alongside ants and yeti
crabs – that farm their food. The little fish don't actually sow seeds, but
let them waft in from surrounding areas, then pull out any unappetizing
seaweeds, leaving only the soft, delicious varieties. It's thought early
humans did a similar thing when they started weeding wild vegetation to
grow edible plants.

The ichthyological farmers go a step further by chasing off intruders
from their farms, each of which can be as big as a ping-pong table. They
even use their mouths to pick up grazing sea urchins by the spines and drop
them some distance away. And it's a good thing they do. When scientists
experimentally keep damselfish away from their farms, it takes trespassers
only a few days to demolish the cultivated crops.

Another aspect of damselfish husbandry has recently come to light.
A team of marine biologists in Belize noticed that many farms of longfin
damselfish (*Stegastes diencaeus*) were occupied by shoals of tiny shrimp, called
mysids. Their hunch was that the shrimp were gaining protection from
predators by hanging out in these well-defended territories. To test this
idea, the scientists put shrimp in plastic bags in various places underwater
and watched to see how often predators tried to eat them. Outside a
damselfish farm, the shrimp were much more likely to be attacked.

Why, then, do damselfish let the shrimp stay, rather than chasing them
off or indeed eating them (damselfish are not strict vegetarians)? Further
studies in Belize revealed that the shrimp release nutrients in their urine
and faeces, which act as a fertilizer for the algae. Divers saw that on farms
with shrimp, the tended algae grow better and the damselfish are healthier
and better fed than those with naturally shrimp-free farms. All this
suggests that damselfish have domesticated the shrimp, keeping shoals like
livestock. It's the first known example, other than humans, of vertebrates
domesticating another animal. It's likely that similar circumstances played
out in the distant past when humans domesticated pigs, cats, chickens and

dogs. Wild animals were attracted to human settlements by food scraps and shelter, and perhaps because people kept predators away. Over time, the animals grew habituated to human presence and both parties found they had something to gain by living together.

There are close to 400 species of damselfish living around the world, mostly on coral reefs. Sergeant majors (*Abudefduf* spp.) show off their stripes, and green chromis (*Chromis viridis*) hang above corals in shimmering shoals. Bright-orange damselfish called Garibaldi (*Hypsypops rubicundus*) live among giant kelp forests along the California coast.

As well as being bold, damselfish are notoriously noisy. They make whooping, popping and chirping sounds by gnashing their teeth together, to flirt with each other and shoo off intruders from their farms. In 2016 divers on the Great Barrier Reef heard Ambon damselfish (*Pomacentrus amboinensis*) making a sound they'd never heard before. The damselfish squeaked like a windscreen wiper. It's likely they adopted a new call to make themselves heard above the racket of a busy reef.

In Indonesia, scientists have been recording the sounds of a coral reef as it recovers from decades of dynamite fishing, in which booming explosives were thrown into the water to kill fish but devastated the entire reef. For years it was silent, but with the help of the coral fragments that scientists have planted out, the ecosystem is growing healthier and noisier. Among the chattering fish voices, scientists recognize the whooping of damselfish.

Seahorse

Hippocampus spp.

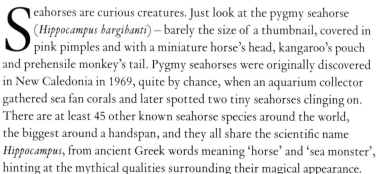

Seahorses are curious creatures. Just look at the pygmy seahorse (*Hippocampus bargibanti*) – barely the size of a thumbnail, covered in pink pimples and with a miniature horse's head, kangaroo's pouch and prehensile monkey's tail. Pygmy seahorses were originally discovered in New Caledonia in 1969, quite by chance, when an aquarium collector gathered sea fan corals and later spotted two tiny seahorses clinging on. There are at least 45 other known seahorse species around the world, the biggest around a handspan, and they all share the scientific name *Hippocampus*, from ancient Greek words meaning 'horse' and 'sea monster', hinting at the mythical qualities surrounding their magical appearance.

People have known of seahorses for a long time, and long wondered what kind of animal they might be. Are they caterpillars, shrimp or miniature, swimming dragons? Fishermen in ancient Greece believed Mediterranean seahorses were the offspring of hippocamps, the fabled beasts with a horse's forelegs and a fish's tail that thundered through the Greek myths pulling Poseidon's chariot. Hippocamps appear on ancient Egyptian sarcophagi and Phoenician coins. They galloped through ancient Roman mythology and on to stone carvings made in the Middle Ages by the Picts of Scotland.

For centuries, dried seahorses have been used in folkloric medicines to treat all sorts of condition, from asthma to broken bones, incontinence to impotence. Still today, seahorse-laced potions command high prices as traditional Chinese medicines. Concerns over unsustainable fishing have led many countries to ban seahorse exports, but still the black market rages on and tens of millions are caught each year, most snagged in shrimp-trawling nets. Consequently, several species are heading for extinction.

As far as Western science is concerned, seahorses contain no potent molecules that would explain their alleged medicinal properties. Despite their supernatural reputation, they are just fish, although unlike any other. Seahorses are the only fish with necks. Instead of a caudal fin to swim with, they have a coiling appendage and a compulsion to hold on to things. Perhaps strangest of all, they are the only animals in which the males become pregnant. Seahorse partners perform elegant courtship rituals, dancing with their tails entwined, after which the female transfers eggs to the male's belly pouch. He then fertilizes them with sperm and begins a two-week gestation, providing the growing young with oxygen and food inside his pouch. In many species, his partner stays faithful, paying daily visits, and they continue dancing to maintain their pair bond. Eventually, he gives birth, huffing and puffing with contractions of his pouch, until a shoal of tiny, fully formed baby seahorses emerges. The young ones have no more help from their parents and drift off to start their own lives.

Seahorses live along most of the world's coastlines, in all but the very coldest seas. Common hang-outs are coral reefs, seagrass meadows and mangrove forests, and they are tricky to spot. Camouflage is a key survival tactic for these slow-swimming fish. They melt out of sight, changing colour and texture to match their surroundings, and wait for prey to come within range, mostly tiny, twitching crustaceans called copepods. With a swift flick of its long snout, a seahorse sucks in its target in a fraction of a millisecond with an 80 per cent hit rate, making these little fish among the world's deadliest predators.

This odd group of fish belongs to an equally eccentric family, the Syngnathidae (from Latin words meaning 'fused jaws', on account of the fact that they all have mouthparts joined into a tube). Members of the family include the seahorses' skinny cousins the pipefish (Syngnathinae), which look like animated bootlaces. Pygmy pipehorses (Hippocampinae) are evolutionarily and anatomically somewhere between seahorses and pipefish. Roaming the coasts of Australia are arguably the three most splendid syngnathid species: the sea dragons. Weedy and leafy seadragons (*Phyllopteryx taeniolatus* and *Phycodurus eques* respectively) hide in kelp forests and seaweed meadows along Australia's southern coast. The striking colour of the ruby seadragons (*Phyllopteryx dewysea*) helps them to hide in deeper waters, where no red light from the sun penetrates to illuminate them so that they appear shadowy and indistinct.

New seahorse species are also being found, such as the honeypot seahorse, *H. nalu*, identified in 2020 from Sodwana Bay, South Africa. In the southern African languages of Xhosa and Zulu, *nalu* means 'here it is', reflecting the fact that these tiny seahorses were there all along, awaiting discovery.

Angelfish and Butterflyfish

Pomacanthidae and *Chaetodontidae*

Among the most colourful and conspicuous inhabitants of coral reefs are the angelfish and butterflyfish. They parade around during the day, often in pairs or flitting together in shoals, and many species are quite brave and unafraid of scuba divers. With their striking patterns of stripes and spots, they are some of the easier fish species to recognize and identify. Some resemble land animals, such as the racoon butterflyfish (*Chaetodon lunula*) with a dark mask over its eyes, or the striped zebra angelfish (*Genicanthus caudovittatus*) and panda butterflyfish (*Chaetodon adiergastos*), with their black eye patches. Others are named for their striking appearance, such as the flame angelfish, teardrop butterflyfish and lemonpeel angelfish (*Centropyge loricula*, *Chaetodon unimaculatus* and *Centropyge flavissima*). Some are simply big and beautiful, with names to match, such as the emperor, queen and king angelfish (*Pomacanthus imperator*, *Holacanthus ciliaris* and *H. passer*).

An obvious explanation for why these animals evolved to be so bright and bold is to announce their identity to each other. Angelfish and butterflyfish are highly territorial and aggressive towards each other. Their brazen 'poster colours', as ichthyologists call them, probably act as displays to stake out territory – like unfurling flags across the reef – and fend off intruders. This could be why young angelfish often look quite different from the adults, and develop their distinctive poster colours only when they grow up and are ready to take over their own territory.

Like their insect namesakes, many butterflyfish have dark spots on their bodies, sometimes ringed in iridescent blue, which could have evolved to look like eyes. Meanwhile, many of them hide their real eyes under a dark band. The false eyes could deflect the attention of predators that might be more likely to strike at the head and eyes of their prey. Predators could also become confused if they think a butterflyfish is looking at them but then it swims off in an unexpected direction.

New technology is helping scientists to discover species of angelfish and butterflyfish in waters that used to be out of reach. Using regular scuba equipment, divers can go safely to only 30 metres (100 ft) underwater. Rebreathing diving equipment lets divers circulate their exhaled bubbles, and with added oxygen they can stay much longer and deeper underwater. That's how diving scientists discovered a new ecological zone on coral reefs, between 30 and 150 metres (100–490 ft) down. They named it the mesophotic ('middle light') zone, because light levels are low although it's not yet the full darkness of the deep sea. In this shadowy realm lives a distinct gathering of corals, sponges, algae and fish, including species of angelfish and butterflyfish that don't live any shallower.

Many angelfish from the mesophotic are rarely seen, such as the Réunion angelfish (*Apolemychthys guezei*), which has been photographed only twice, and the humbug-like red-striped peppermint angelfish of Rarotonga (*Centropyge boylei*), for which aquarium keepers have apparently offered huge sums of money. A few years ago, divers collected a live butterflyfish from a mesophotic reef in the Philippines. It was only when they took it to the United States for an aquarium exhibition at the California Academy of Sciences that they realized the species hadn't been described before. They named it *Roa rumsfeldi* after the American politician Donald Rumsfeld, who spoke of how in war there are the known unknowns, as well as unknown unknowns, the ones we don't know we don't know. This little butterflyfish, hiding out on the deep, mesophotic reefs, is one of many ichthyological unknown unknowns that are gradually coming to light.

Back in the shallows, butterflyfish are important indicators of the health of coral reefs. Many species feed only on coral polyps, delicately nibbling at them, so they thrive only in areas where there's plenty of living coral. Counting butterflyfish can be a useful way of gauging how well a reef ecosystem is doing: the more butterflyfish, the healthier the corals.

CARIBBEAN

Queen Conch

Aliger gigas

For millennia, people across the Caribbean have eaten queen conch and used the shells as decorations and tools. The Aztec god Quetzalcóatl is depicted wearing a 'wind jewel' made from a conch shell sliced in two. Conch shells were left as offerings in Aztec graves and used as inlay in ornaments, often alongside red spiny oyster shells. Mayan carvings depict people fighting with conch shells in their hands, using them like boxing gloves. Mayans also used conch shells as ceremonial trumpets.

Like many large sea-snail shells, a queen conch shell can be fashioned into a musical instrument by cutting off the tip and blowing into it. Air vibrates and resonates inside the shell's large, hollow cavity, creating a relatively tuneful note, in a similar way to a brass instrument. The physics of shell trumpets also explains the old story that if you hold a shell to your ear you can hear the sound of the sea. What you're hearing is in fact the amplified and resonating sound of blood whooshing through your ears, and other ambient noises. Trumpets are also traditionally made from other sea-snail species around the world, including triton shells (*Charonia tritonis*) in the Pacific islands, and the divine conch (*Turbinella pyrum*) used by Buddhist monks in the Himalayas.

Conch shells continue to be a favourite of collectors around the world. They've also been popular for making cameos, oval jewellery carved with a person's profile. Immense piles of conch shells are evidence that people have eaten a lot of these snails. Consequently, living conch have become a rare sight across seagrass meadows in the Caribbean Sea, the Gulf of Mexico and northeastern Brazil.

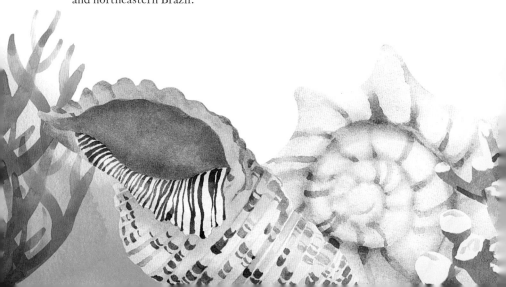

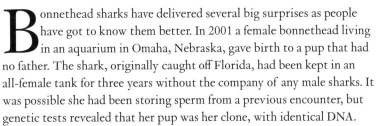

Bonnethead Shark

Sphyrna tiburo

Bonnethead sharks have delivered several big surprises as people have got to know them better. In 2001 a female bonnethead living in an aquarium in Omaha, Nebraska, gave birth to a pup that had no father. The shark, originally caught off Florida, had been kept in an all-female tank for three years without the company of any male sharks. It was possible she had been storing sperm from a previous encounter, but genetic tests revealed that her pup was her clone, with identical DNA.

The process by which an egg develops directly into an embryo without being fertilized by sperm is known as parthenogenesis. It can happen in various animals, including snakes, salamanders, insects, snails and spiders. But the bonnethead shark was the first shark to display this behaviour, which presumably evolved as a way for animals to reproduce during times when mates are hard to come by. Since the bonnethead 'virgin birth', several other shark species have reproduced in aquariums via parthenogenesis, among them white-spotted bamboo sharks (*Chiloscyllium plagiosum*), blacktip sharks (*Carcharhinus limbatus*) and zebra sharks (*Stegostoma tigrinum*).

Bonnetheads have shown that not all sharks are bloodthirsty carnivores. In fact, some eat grass. In the past, when people saw bonnethead sharks in the wild chomping mouthfuls of seagrass they generally assumed this was merely accidental and that the sharks were lunging for their target prey of crabs, shrimp, fish and snails. A team of scientists decided to investigate. They kept several bonnethead sharks in an aquarium with squid and seagrass to eat. Then a series of tests revealed that the sharks are true omnivores. They don't have the kind of teeth that can chew seagrass, but they swallow great chunks whole, and these may be broken down by strong stomach acids. The sharks have in their stomach enzymes that help them to digest tough plant material. Chemical analysis revealed that seagrass made up more than half of the bonnetheads' diet.

The finding casts sharks in a whole new light, and shows that seagrass meadows are not only important habitat for turtles, dugongs and various invertebrates and smaller fish, but also critical for sharks. In addition, it suggests that scientists would do well to pay more attention to the diet of other animals that are assumed to be diehard meat-eaters.

Various ideas have been proposed to explain why bonnetheads and the other hammerhead sharks have such bizarrely wide heads. The cephalofoils,

as they're known, may give them extra lift and manoeuvrability. There is also a large surface area for sense organs that detect smells and weak electric signals from prey hiding in the seabed. With their wide-set eyes, hammerhead sharks also have enhanced binocular vision, helping them to track and chase prey.

Narwhal

Monodon monoceros

Among the regalia Queen Elizabeth I kept in the Jewel Room in the Tower of London were various objects made from the horns of unicorns. A surviving inventory notes a unicorn cup and several sceptres fashioned from unicorn horns and adorned with silver and crystals. Historians think the Queen may have collected these objects as symbols celebrating her unusual status as an unmarried female monarch, since it was said that unicorns could be captured only by virgins.

For centuries there was a lucrative international commerce in 'unicorn horns'. Across medieval Europe, people widely believed that drinking from a cup made of unicorn horn protected against any poison. Spiders placed inside the cup would indicate its authenticity, if they quickly curled up their legs and died. For people who couldn't afford an expensive cup, a sprinkling of ground unicorn horn guarded against a range of medical complaints.

It is easy to look back and chuckle at the gullible folk paying good money for these made-up drugs, but they arose in times when great mysteries lingered, much of the world remained unexplored, and no one knew for sure whether or not these animals really existed. In time it emerged that Danish merchants had been gathering these horns from the seas around Greenland by pulling out the elongated, spiral buckteeth from medium-sized whales called narwhals.

Long after the unicorn horn's true identity was revealed, a great mystery still surrounds the tusks of narwhals. No one is quite sure why narwhals have tusks, or what they use them for. It's difficult to be sure, because they are highly elusive animals that spend a good deal of their lives hidden under Arctic sea ice. Various theories have been proposed. Maybe the tusks make or detect sounds. They could be tools for digging out food from the seabed or for breaking up sea ice to make breathing holes. They could be giant sensors for detecting chemicals and temperature changes in the water, an idea that is backed up by the presence of nerve connections in the tusk and channels that allow seawater to flow in.

A snag in all these theories is the fact that female narwhals are usually tuskless. Whatever benefit the dental adornment serves, it's something that only the males gain from. A recent study lent support to the idea that tusks are the narwhal equivalent of a red deer's enormous rack of antlers or a peacock's outrageous tail. Male narwhals could have evolved tusks to do battle with each other and show off to females. And, as is often the case in the animal kingdom, the bigger the better. Male narwhals have been found covered in scars and with broken tusks. There are also reported cases of 'tusking', where two narwhals rub tusks together.

In the cold waters of the Arctic, narwhals live alongside their close relatives the beluga whales (*Delphinapterus leucas*). The latter are known as the canaries of the sea because of their chirping voices, which is one reason belugas have been so popular for putting on display in aquariums, a practice that more people are recognizing as being unnecessary and cruel.

In 2019 a beluga whale appeared off the Norwegian coastal town of Hammerfest, a long way south of the species' normal range. Even more strangely, it was wearing a harness adorned with the words 'Equipment St Petersburg'. Was it an escaped Russian spy? It's been reported that a few years previously the Russian navy was training belugas, seals and dolphins to guard the entrances of naval bases and kill underwater intruders. Allegedly, however, belugas are not as good as seals at taking orders. The Russian beluga, named Hvaldimir (a mixture of the Norwegian word for whale, *hval*, and the Russian president, Vladimir Putin), stayed near Hammerfest, approaching people for company, and sleeping and feeding near salmon farms. Campaigners want a fjord to be cordoned off to keep Hvaldimir from harm.

Antarctic Icefish

Notothenioidei

In the icy seas surrounding Antarctica live fish that don't freeze. Even though they swim through water at temperatures as low as −1.9°C (28.6°F), these cold-blooded animals don't turn into fish Popsicles. For a long while scientists puzzled over this and predicted that the fish must have some kind of ice-inhibiting mechanism. Then, in the 1960s, their secret came to light. It turns out that Antarctic icefish fill their bodies with antifreeze.

The substance is a simple protein made in an icefish's pancreas. It binds to ice crystals that enter the body, including any the fish eats, and stops them from growing any bigger. The fish then gets rid of the trapped ice crystals in its faeces. Icefish also smear their skin with mucus laced with antifreeze proteins to stop themselves from getting a frosty overcoat. Following the original discovery of natural antifreezes in Antarctic icefish, scientists began examining other organisms that live in sub-zero conditions and have found lots of other ice-halting molecules, in trees and grasses, beetles, snow fleas, moths and plankton. Atlantic herring, sea ravens and winter flounder are among various other ice-proof fish. Antarctic icefish and Arctic cod are distant relatives that live on opposite sides of the planet, and yet they make an almost identical form of antifreeze proteins. Antarctic icefish evolved theirs from a digestive enzyme. In contrast, Arctic cod evolved their antifreeze from part of their genome that doesn't normally code for anything – the so-called junk DNA.

Various ideas have sprung up for using antifreeze proteins in the human world. Cryopreservation is one possibility; natural antifreezes could help to safely store donated organs, blood cells, sperm and embryos. We might one day see environmentally friendly anti-frost coatings on overhead power lines and aeroplane wings. And already antifreeze proteins are used by the food industry, somewhat counterintuitively to make ice cream. By preventing large ice crystals from forming, antifreeze proteins apparently make a deliciously smooth product. But you won't see anything fishy on the list of ingredients. Look out instead for 'ice structuring proteins'. Ice-cream makers decided to avoid any confusion with ethylene glycol, the antifreeze used in car de-icers, which is highly toxic.

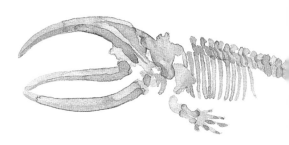

Bowhead Whale

Balaena mysticetus

owhead whales hold an impressive collection of world records.
They have the biggest mouth of any animal, at 5 metres (16 ft)
long, 4 metres (13 ft) high and 2.5 metres wide (8 ft), which is big
enough to house a 1-tonne tongue. And they live for longer than any other
mammals. In 2007 Iñupiat people in Alaska killed a bowhead whale as part
of their subsistence hunt, and the whale already had the head of a harpoon
lodged deep in its blubber. The harpoon was of a design made only between
1879 and 1885, so someone had tried – and failed – to kill this whale a long
time before, and the animal had swum around with a harpoon in its blubber
for more than a century. Scientists have estimated that bowhead whales can
live for at least 200 years, although many haven't had the chance.

Commercial hunting for bowheads started in the eighteenth century.
They are slow, easy targets and conveniently float when harpooned. Like
other whales, bowheads were killed for their oil to burn in lamps and make
into soap, lipstick and glue. Their pliable baleen plates, which the whales
use to strain water for food, were used to make corsets and brushes. By
the turn of the twentieth century European and American whalers had
hunted bowheads almost to extinction. But since 1982, when commercial
whale hunting was banned, numbers have increased. In the western Arctic,
bowheads have gone from around a thousand individuals to at least 16,800
with the help of native communities, such as the Iñupiat, who monitor
and study their populations and fight against offshore oil drilling and
other impacts.

Bowheads are the only whales that live full-time in the Arctic, and
they're well adapted to survive in icy seas. They use their huge heads to
break through sea ice so that they can breathe. They are also much chubbier
than other whale species, with blubber half a metre thick. This gives them
such effective insulation that they risk overheating when migrating on long
journeys. To cool themselves, bowheads open their mouths and let cold
seawater pour over a special rod of soft, spongy tissue in the roof of their
mouth. Blood flows into this organ – which whale biologists liken to a penis
– making it swell up and stiffen.

During the dark Arctic winters, bowhead whales sing to each other.
Scientists have placed a hydrophone between Greenland and Svalbard,
and recorded them singing non-stop, 24 hours a day, between November

and April each year. They have an ever-changing repertoire of moaning, swooping songs. Compared to the other great singers, the humpback whales, they are not so much classical musicians as free jazz improvisers. Scientists have yet to unravel why bowheads sing these free-form songs, but it probably has something to do with mating.

Greenland Shark

Somniosus microcephalus

O f all the animals with backbones, Greenland sharks live the
longest. We know this because of a secret they've been keeping in
their eyes.

Greenland sharks don't have hard parts in their bodies that let you
count their years, such as ear bones (otoliths) that show annual growth
patterns like tree rings. Instead, scientists gaze into the middle of a
Greenland shark's eyes at the parts that were laid down when it was just a
pup. Chemical analysis of the eyes of sharks caught incidentally in fisheries
reveals that some have a radioactive marker that coincides with the nuclear
weapons tests from the 1950s and 1960s, placing their birth year at around
the same time. From those, it's possible to work out the age of older, bigger
sharks. The oldest tested so far was a female who was 392, give or take a
century. She probably mated for the first time when she was 156 years old.

Greenland sharks are dopey giants, growing to more than 5 metres
(16 ft) long and swimming through Arctic and North Atlantic waters, at
speeds slower than 1.6 kilometres (1 mile) an hour. They were once targeted
for their liver oil, which is rich in vitamin A. Some are still used for their
meat, which contains so much urea it's toxic to eat without special handling.
Hákarl is a national dish in Iceland made from fermented Greenland shark.
Traditionally, the meat is buried under stones to rot for a few months, then
hung up to dry for a few months longer. The end product is eaten in small
cubes and stinks of ammonia. Pinching your nose is recommended, as is
following it with a shot of the strong Icelandic spirit *brennivín*.

Greenland Halibut

Reinhardtius hippoglossoides

The Greenland halibut looks like a fish that can't make up its mind. It belongs to the Pleuronectidae, the righteye flounders, that generally spend their lives lying on the seabed left side down, gazing upwards with both eyes on the right-hand side of their face. They don't start out that way, though. As larvae, flounders have eyes like those of most other fish, one on each side of their head. But when they are a few weeks old, one eye wanders off and moves across their face to join the other. Then the fish tips over and lies flat. But in Greenland halibut, the roaming eye goes only halfway, then stops in the middle of its forehead, turning it into the ichthyological cousin of a Cyclops. This leaves them with the option of either lying and swimming on their side or swimming in a vertical position. These are part-time flatfish. They're also fish that nearly sparked a war.

In 1995 Canada and Spain almost came to blows over the fishing of Greenland halibut. Canadian fisheries were in ruins after the collapse of the Grand Banks cod fishery off the Newfoundland coast. Desperate for alternative fish to catch, the Canadians turned their nets towards the halibut and introduced strict quotas to avoid a repeat of the devastating collapse of cod. But trawlers from the European Union were also coming over to nearby waters and catching far more halibut. Canadian fishermen were convinced the halibut they were trying to safeguard were being over-fished by everyone else.

Matters came to a head when a Canadian navy vessel chased a Spanish factory-freezer trawler and fired machine guns across its bow, before arresting the crew and seizing the vessel. Canadian officials discovered the Spanish fishers were using illegal nets and hiding illegal catches in secret storage tanks on board. The incident escalated as more naval vessels and air patrols piled in, and it looked as though real combat would break out. Eventually, Spain agreed to leave the disputed zone and Canada returned the impounded Spanish trawler.

Fishing for Greenland halibut continues more peacefully these days, although problems may lie ahead. Around Greenland, where halibut is the basis of an important industry, the best catches come from areas where glaciers run along fjords and right into the sea. Deep meltwater from the glaciers stirs up nutrients and stimulates the growth of plankton, boosting the entire food web. Scientists predict that as the climate warms, glaciers will retreat on to land; without the meltwater the nutrient cycles will probably weaken and populations of Greenland halibut will move away and decline.

In the same cold waters, another species of righteye flounder is the Atlantic halibut (*Hippoglossus hippoglossus*), a giant that can measure close to 5 metres (16 ft) long and weigh hundreds of kilograms. They're a favourite food of Greenland sharks. Righteye flounders that people like to eat include various species of sole, turbot and plaice.

There are also flatfish that lie on the other side. Lefteye flounders (Bothidae) include the peacock flounders (*Bothus mancus*), which live in tropical waters and are covered in gleaming blue circles. They can change colour and pattern quickly to match their surroundings, a key tactic for flatfish. They lie down and hope not to be seen, either by predators or by potential prey.

There are great advantages to being good at hiding and lying flat on the seabed. Stingrays do it in a different way, flattening themselves like a pancake, from belly to back. But the way flatfish have done it makes them the most asymmetrical vertebrates on the planet. Scientists recently discovered that flatfish became very weird very fast. Every time a young flatfish grows up and its eye moves, it's retracing an evolutionary journey that took around 3 million years – not long, considering all the changes to their skull that make their flat lives possible.

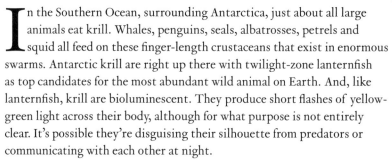

Antarctic Krill

Euphausia superba

In the Southern Ocean, surrounding Antarctica, just about all large animals eat krill. Whales, penguins, seals, albatrosses, petrels and squid all feed on these finger-length crustaceans that exist in enormous swarms. Antarctic krill are right up there with twilight-zone lanternfish as top candidates for the most abundant wild animal on Earth. And, like lanternfish, krill are bioluminescent. They produce short flashes of yellow-green light across their body, although for what purpose is not entirely clear. It's possible they're disguising their silhouette from predators or communicating with each other at night.

Krill range over a huge swathe of habitat, covering roughly 10 per cent of the global ocean, roughly the area of the African continent. This makes it difficult to measure exactly how abundant they are, but estimates suggest there's somewhere around 500 million tonnes (0.5 gigatonnes), a similar biomass to all the humans or cows on Earth.

As well as being at the heart of the Southern Ocean food web, krill play a vital role in the climate. They feed on minute algae called phytoplankton in the surface seas and produce large, dense droppings that are full of carbon and rapidly sink. The krill also swim down daily into deeper waters, to try to avoid all those hungry predators, and release more carbon into the water as they exhale. In total, krill draw down tens of millions of tonnes of carbon into the deep sea every year, where it can stay for millennia locked away from the atmosphere.

Whales and penguins aren't the only species that krill need to worry about; people are also major predators of these prolific crustaceans. Industrial factory ships can catch as much as 800 tonnes of krill a day. Enormous nets pump up krill continuously and stay in the water for weeks at a time. The catches are then processed right away on the ship and mashed down to make krill-oil pills that are rich in omega-3 fatty acids. Krill is also turned into fish meal, meaning that animals around the world, a long way from the Southern Ocean, also feed on it. Livestock, farmed fish and pet cats and dogs all eat krill.

Conservationists are concerned about the effect of fishing on krill. For now, it's unlikely the species as a whole will suffer, but studies suggest that local populations can be hit hard, which reduces the food available to predators, including penguins that don't swim far to forage while they are nesting and rearing their chicks. Climate change is also a great threat to krill. They rely for part of their life cycle on sea ice, which in some places is swiftly shrinking as the Southern Ocean warms.

Where to go next

Now that you've met 80 of the ocean's inhabitants, there are many ways you can continue your search for oceanic life.

Explore the coast

If you're lucky enough to live near a coastline or you have a chance to visit, take time to explore and find out what's there. Coastal habitats to head for include:

Rocky shores
These are the perfect place to encounter marine life on foot. All you need is a pair of wellies or shoes you don't mind getting wet. Check the tide times (search for local tide tables online) and head out an hour or so before low tide. This will give you access to the parts of the shore that are submerged for longest and are home to some of the most oceanic animals you can see while still walking on land.

Search under rocks for sea snails, fish, sea urchins and starfish, and look in rock pools for shrimp and fish that get temporarily trapped when the tide goes out. Always be careful to put rocks back where you found them. Watch where you tread, for your own sake (sea-urchin spines can go through boots) and for the ecosystem.

Rocky shores can also be a great place to snorkel at high tide. I recommend wearing a wetsuit to protect you from scratches and cold.

As you explore a coastline, you will start to notice variations in wildlife from place to place. Shores exposed to waves and storms tend to have fewer species and be dominated by animals that cling tightly to rocks, such as limpets, barnacles and mussels. More sheltered shores generally have a greater variety of animals, and more seaweed. This is where you'll find more crabs and sea snails.

Sandy beaches

Low tide is the best time to explore stretches of sand and see what the sea has thrown up, especially after a storm.

You will probably find lots of empty shells of clams and other bivalves that live burrowed in the sand.

Look out for the internal shells of cuttlefish, known as cuttlebones. Keep an eye out for shark and skate egg cases, also known as mermaid's purses. You should be able to work out which species you've found from the shape and size of the case.

Clifftops

From up high, you'll get an excellent view across the sea, so cliffs are a good vantage point for spotting larger marine animals such as dolphins, whales, seabirds and large sharks, such as basking sharks. Bring a pair of binoculars.

Encounters with marine megafauna

There are many boat-based opportunities to have enthralling close encounters with large marine animals, such as whales, dolphins and basking sharks. Before joining a trip, do some research into the species of interest and make sure your tour operator abides by any ethical and safely guidelines. Be sure to respect the animals in their wild home; don't get too close, don't be noisy and definitely don't touch.

Going deeper

If you're tempted to explore the deeper parts of the sea, you can learn to scuba dive or free dive.

Scuba

Various organizations offer scuba certification programmes, including a chance to try diving with an instructor first, to see how you like it. Entry-level courses generally last a week or so, and if you really get hooked you can keep going, advancing your skill all the way up to divemaster and dive instructor.

Check out:

British Sub-Aqua Club:
www.bsac.com/home
National Association of Underwater Instructors: www.naui.org
Professional Association of Diving Instructors: www.padi.com
Scuba Schools International:
www.divessi.com
World Underwater Federation:
www.cmas.org

Free diving

Free diving, or apnoea, requires less equipment but more skill as you swim down holding your breath. A few days' training will show you the basics and important safety techniques (never free dive on your own, for example), and soon you'll be holding your breath and going deeper than you ever thought you could.

Check out:

Apnea Academy/Apnea Academy International: www.apnea.academy
International Association for the Development of Apnea:
www.aidainternational.org

Online resources

MarLIN (The Marine Life Information Network): www.marlin.ac.uk/species
Ocean Life at the Smithsonian: www.ocean.si.edu/ocean-life
Oceana Marine Life Encyclopedia: www.oceana.org/marine-life

How to protect ocean life

Despite the many threats bearing down on ocean life, the good news is that there are many excellent people and organizations around the world working hard to halt and reverse the problems, and bring the ocean back to its full, glorious health. Here are a few of them:

Blue Marine Foundation
www.bluemarinefoundation.com
Working on developing ways to tackle unsustainable fishing and restore marine habitats, such as oyster reefs, with an overarching mission to protect at least 30 per cent of the world's ocean by 2030.

Deep Sea Conservation Coalition
www.savethehighseas.org
More than 100 NGOs, fisher organizations, law and policy institutes around the world working to protect vulnerable deep-sea ecosystems from impacts such as deep-sea trawling and seabed mining.

Mission Blue
www.mission-blue.org
Led by the legendary American oceanographer Sylvia Earle, Mission Blue's aim is to create an upwelling of public awareness, access and support for a worldwide network of marine protected areas across the world, called Hope Spots – special places scientifically identified as critical to the health of the ocean.

Seasearch
www.seasearch.org.uk
A project for recreational divers and snorkellers in the United Kingdom and Ireland who want to do their bit for the marine environment by collecting information about the marine habitats, plants and animals they see under the water.

Surfers Against Sewage
www.sas.org.uk
A grassroots environmental charity that inspires, unites and empowers communities to take action to protect oceans, beaches, waves and wildlife.

Sustainable Oceans Alliance
www.soalliance.org
Working to mobilize a global ocean workforce of young people to develop and implement innovative solutions to restore the health of the ocean.

Eat sustainable seafood

When it comes to eating seafood, there are better choices to make for the health of the ocean. There are fisheries that are working hard to have as little long-term environmental impact as possible, by targeting species that reproduce quickly, using low-impact fishing gear and staying well within catch limits to avoid pushing wild populations into decline. Some farmed fish and shellfish are also good options.

The snag when eating seafood is that it's not always easy to know what exactly is on your plate, where it came from and how it was caught. You need to know all that in order to be assured how sustainable – or not – your food is. Scrutinize labels, ask fishmongers, supermarkets and restaurant owners how they source their fish, and don't be fobbed off by vague statements about sustainability. Look out for supplies that come from small fisheries that can trace their produce from ocean to plate. Support fisheries you know and trust. Learn about the main species of fish on sale in your region and use online seafood guides to find out what are the most sustainable options.

Check out:
Good Fish Guide: www.mcsuk.org/goodfishguide
GoodFish: www.goodfish.org.au
Seafood Watch: www.seafoodwatch.org

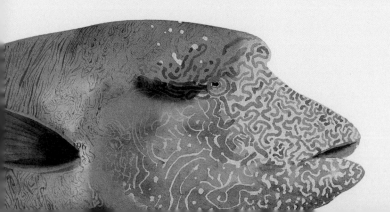

Index

About the author

Dr Helen Scales is a marine biologist, writer and broadcaster. Her studies of the ocean have taken her from the mangroves of Madagascar and the remote coral reefs of Borneo to West African oyster forests and the deep waters of the Gulf of Mexico. Her books include *Spirals in Time: The Secret Life and Curious Afterlife of Seashells* (2015), which was shortlisted for the Royal Society of Biology Book Award, and the *Daily Telegraph*'s science book of the year, *The Brilliant Abyss: True Tales of Exploring the Deep Sea, Discovering Hidden Life and Selling the Seabed* (2021). Her ocean-based writing appears in *National Geographic*, *The Guardian*, *New Scientist* and others. Helen appears regularly on BBC radio; she teaches at the University of Cambridge, advises the ocean conservation charity Sea Changers and is a storytelling ambassador at the Save Our Seas Foundation. She divides her time between Cambridge, UK, and the Atlantic coast of France.
www.helenscales.com

Author's acknowledgements

It has been a tremendous pleasure to have the chance to add a purely oceanic title to this amazing series of books. My great thanks to everyone at Laurence King who has helped to make it happen. Andrew Roff first asked me if I thought there would be enough ocean-going animals to lead us on a journey around the world, and he was brilliant in helping me whittle down the long list of species I came up with. Katherine Pitt smoothly took over the helm of this ocean-going vessel of a book and deftly steered it home through its global journey. Marcel George, thank you for weaving your artwork so beautifully around my words. It's been a great joy to watch this book coming to life on the page.

There are so many people who have taught me about ocean life and continue to do so every day – far too many of you to name, but thank you all. My eternal love and thanks to all my friends and family, who have always been there for me and cheered me on as I've set off to explore the ocean, in person and in words. And Ivan, thank you for sharing your life with me above, on and below the waves.